MAGIC CUBES
New Recreations

MAGIC CUBES
New Recreations

William H. Benson
and Oswald Jacoby

Dover Publications, Inc.
New York

To Ann
in grateful appreciation of
her constant encouragement and
support, without which this book
would never have been written
W. H. B.

Published in Canada by General Publishing Company, Ltd.,
30 Lesmill Road, Don Mills, Toronto, Ontario.
Published in the United Kingdom by Constable and Company, Ltd., 10 Orange Street, London WC2H 7EG.

Magic Cubes: New Recreations is a new work, first published by
Dover Publications, Inc., in 1981.

International Standard Book Number: 0-486-24140-8
Library of Congress Catalog Card Number: 80-70941

Manufactured in the United States of America
Dover Publications, Inc.
180 Varick Street
New York, N.Y. 10014

Preface

This book is for both the newcomer to the field of recreational mathematics, who will not need any previous experience or knowledge of advanced mathematics to enjoy magic cubes, and longstanding magic-cube enthusiasts, who we hope will be interested in the many original sections of the book. The book is in two parts. First we discuss and construct various types of magic cubes and reconstruct the first magic cube ever published. (It was first published over a century ago.) Detailed instructions and examples are given for every type of magic cube. We also include two significant original magic cubes: the first doubly-even-order perfect magic cube of the 12 × 12 × 12 order, and the first singly-even-order perfect magic cube of the 14 × 14 × 14 order. In Part II we give a mathematical proof of the procedures followed in Part I.

Our thanks to Martin Gardner, Thomas W. Burnett, and E. Robert Paul for their interest and helpful suggestions.

Contents

Part I

The World Of Magic Cubes

Chapter 1

Introduction

Most of our readers are probably familiar with magic squares—both the squares that meet the minimum requirements (a square array formed of the positive integers 1 to N^2, inclusive, arranged so that the sum of the integers forming any column, row, or main diagonal is the same) and those that also meet various additional magic requirements. For the most part, there are standard terms to describe these various properties, but rather than attempt to discuss them here, we shall adopt the general policy of defining any term whose meaning is not self-evident the first time it appears in this book.

For magic cubes the situation is different. Martin Gardner makes the following distinctions:

> A perfect magic cube is a cubical array of positive integers from 1 to N^3 such that every straight line of N cells adds up to a constant. These lines include the orthogonals (the lines parallel to an edge), the two main diagonals of every orthogonal cross section and the four space diagonals. The constant is $(1 + 2 + 3 + \cdots + N^3)/N^2 = \frac{1}{2}(N^4 + N)$.

....

Annoyed by the refusal of such a cube to exist (a perfect magic cube of order three), magic cube buffs have relaxed the requirements to define a species of semiperfect cube that apparently does exist in all orders higher than two. These are cubes where only the orthogonals and four space diagonals are magic. Let us call them Andrews cubes, since W. S. Andrews devotes two chapters to them in his work *Magic Squares and Cubes*. ... The order-3 Andrews cube must be associative, with 14 as its center. John R. Hendricks has proved (*Journal of Mathematical Recreational Mathematics*, Vol. 5, January, 1972, pages 43–50) that there are four such cubes, not counting rotations and reflections. All are given by Andrews, although he seems not to have realized that they exhaust all basic types.[1]

Throughout the remainder of this book we shall refer to them simply as *magic cubes*.

In addition let us define a *pandiagonal magic cube* as a magic cube that will remain magic when any orthogonal section (that is, any plane section parallel to one of the faces of the cube) is moved parallel to itself from the front to the back (top to the bottom, or left-hand to right-hand side) of the cube, or the reverse. We will call a perfect magic cube that remains perfect under transpositions of any orthogonal section a *pandiagonal perfect magic cube*.

Gardner correctly notes that Andrews' work is a most interesting book on magic squares and cubes,[2] but there are other important early writings as well. The eleventh edition of W. W. R. Ball's *Mathematical Recreations and Essays* was first printed in 1939 and contains a section on magic cubes that did not appear in the tenth edition.[3] J. Barkley Rosser and Robert J. Walker treat diabolic (pandiagonal perfect) magic cubes in their Supplement to *The Algebraic Theory of Diabolic Magic Squares*.[4] The most surprising of the early writings on magic squares and cubes is F. A. P. Barnard's article.[5] It is astonishing how completely such a remarkable piece has been forgotten, but we hope to do justice to Barnard later in this book.

The following are the various types of possible magic cubes of different orders.

1. Martin Gardner, "Mathematical Games," *Scientific American* (January 1976), pp. 120, 122.

2. W. S. Andrews, *Magic Squares and Cubes: With Chapters by Other Writers*, 2nd ed. rev. (1917; reprint ed., New York: Dover Publications, 1960).

3. W. W. R. Ball, *Mathematical Recreations and Essays*, 11th ed. (New York: Macmillan, 1939), pp. 217–221.

4. J. Barkley Rosser and Robert J. Walker, "The Algebraic Theory of Diabolic Magic Squares: Supplement," (Ithaca, New York: Cornell University Library, n.d.), pp. 740–741.

5. F. A. P. Barnard, "Theory of Magic Squares and of Magic Cubes," in *The Memoirs of the National Academy of Science*, 4 (1888):209–270.

ODD CUBES

$3 \times 3 \times 3$	Magic only
$5 \times 5 \times 5$	Pandiagonal only
$7 \times 7 \times 7$	Pandiagonal or perfect but not both simultaneously
$9 \times 9 \times 9$ and up	Pandiagonal perfect

SINGLY-EVEN

$6 \times 6 \times 6$	Magic only
$10 \times 10 \times 10$	Pandiagonal only
$14 \times 14 \times 14$ and up	Pandiagonal or perfect (if N is prime to 3) but not both simultaneously

DOUBLY-EVEN

$4 \times 4 \times 4$	Pandiagonal only
$12 \times 12 \times 12$ and up	Pandiagonal or perfect but not both simultaneously

TRIPLY-EVEN

$8 \times 8 \times 8$ and up	Pandiagonal perfect

The singly-even and doubly-even perfect magic cubes and the singly-even pandiagonal magic cubes described later are the first of their kind ever to be constructed.

Chapter 2

Third-Order Magic Cubes

With some exceptions to be discussed later, the three-dimension vectors method is unquestionably the most effective way to construct magic cubes. Thus in this chapter we will expand our discussion of the two-dimension cyclical method in *New Recreations With Magic Squares* (see Appendix) to three dimensions, paying particular attention to the requirements to be met. Let us identify the order of the cube as N.

As a first step we shall identify the individual cells forming the cube by the coordinates (x,y,z), where x, y, and z equal 0, 1, 2, 3, . . . , $(N-1)$, counting from the left to the right (x), from the bottom up (y), and from the front to the back (z).

Since we are using cyclical steps, all coordinates that differ by an exact multiple of N are equivalent. Thus the cell [13,8,6] would be equivalent to cell [3,3,1] in a fifth-order cube and to cell [5,0,6] in an eighth-order cube. More generally we see that if u, v, and w are integers (positive or negative or zero, not necessarily different) then the cell $[x+uN,\ y+vN,\ z+wN]$ is equivalent to cell $[x,y,z]$.

As a matter of convenience, we shall operate with the numbers 0 to (N^3-1) rather than the numbers 1 to N^3. This involves no loss in generality inasmuch as we can always convert our modified cube into a standard one by adding 1 to the number in each cell of the cube. Also, we will frequently express numbers to the base N, that is, we shall express numbers as xN^2+XN+x, where x, X, and x each take on any possible value from 0 to $(N-1)$.

The second step is to select nine integers—C, R, D, c, r, d, *c*, *r*, and *d* (positive, negative, or zero, and not necessarily different)—such that:

(1) Each integer is greater than $-N$ and less than $+N$.
(2) No more than one capital, lowercase, or italic letter is 0.
(3) No more than one letter c, r, or d, is 0.
(4) The following determinant is prime to N. (Two integers are prime to each other when they have no common factor greater than 1; it follows that 1 is prime to all other integers). As far as this requirement is concerned, the sign of the determinant is immaterial.

$$\Delta = - \begin{vmatrix} C & R & D \\ c & r & d \\ c & r & d \end{vmatrix}$$

(5) None of the controlling characteristics for *x*, X, and x in the orthogonals (that is, the series of N cells parallel to any of the edges) is equal to 0. (This requirement will be clarified later.)

For simplicity we shall hereafter refer to such a cube of order N as the

$$\begin{vmatrix} C & R & D \\ c & r & d \\ c & r & d \end{vmatrix}_N \quad \text{cube}$$

In order to demonstrate this method in detail let us consider the following cube as Case 1:

$$\begin{vmatrix} 1 & 1 & 0 \\ 1 & 0 & 1 \\ 0 & 1 & 1 \end{vmatrix}_N$$

That is, in Case 1 C = 1, R = 1, D = 0, c = 1, r = 0, d = 1, *c* = 0, *r* = 1, and *d* = 1, and $\Delta = 2$.

Once the various constants have been selected the construction is acqually quite simple. The easiest way to explain it is with an example. We shall first construct a third-order magic cube using the values given in Case 1. Note particularly that these values, as well as that of Δ, meet requirements 1 to 4 inclusive when *N* equals 3.

A unique feature of our method is that, regardless of the order of the cube, a very general intermediate cube is first constructed with the aid of three series of letters, namely,

$$A, B, C, D, \ldots, N,$$

$$a, b, c, d, \ldots, n, \text{ and}$$

$$a, b, c, d, \ldots, n.$$

The next step in the actual construction of our cube is to generate this intermediate cube by the use of one series of cyclical steps after another. Each individual cell is occupied by one of these triplets of letters in accordance with the following rules (as long as requirement (4) is met, no triplet will fall in a cell already occupied by another triplet. See proof in Chapter 13.):

(1)   The *a*A series is started by placing the triplet *a*Aa in any desired cell, say cell [2,2,2].

(2)   The remaining triplets in the *a*A series are located by taking a series of construction steps, which we shall identify as the (C,R,D) *regular* (or *lowercase*) *step,* consisting of C columns to the right (left when C is negative), R rows up (down when R is negative), and D cells back (forward when D is negative) from the last cell filled. For Case 1, C = 1, R = 1, and D = 0, so this regular step is one cell to the right and one cell up in the same plane (since D is 0). This will place *a*Ab in cell [3,3,2], or what is the equivalent, in cell [0,0,2], and *a*Ac in cell [1,1,2]. Note that if you attempt to make one more regular step, the next cell [2,2,2] is already occupied by the number *a*Aa.

(3)   It is evident that a special move (which we shall refer to as the *capital letter cross-step*) is necessary to start the *a*B series. This cross-step, which we shall identify as the (C+c, R+r, D+d) cross-step, consists of (C+c) columns to the right (left when (C+c) is negative), (R+r) rows up (down when (R+r) is negative), and (D+d) cells back (forward when (D+d) is neg-

ative). For Case 1, this consists of (C+C) = two cells to the right, (R+r) = one row up, and (D+d) = one cell back. It follows that aBa belongs in cell [3,2,3], or what is the equivalent, in cell [0,2,0].

(4) After the first capital letter cross-step has enabled us to locate the first triplet in the aB series, we return to the regular lowercase step of one cell to the right and one cell up in the same plane and continue until the aB series is completed. This will place the number aBb in cell [1,3,0], or what is the equivalent, in cell [1,0,0], and the number aBc in cell [2,1,0].

(5) Once more we are blocked and therefore return to the capital letter cross-step to start the aC series. This will place the number aCa in cell [4,2,1] or what is its equivalent, in cell [1,2,1].

(6) After the second capital letter cross-step has enabled us to locate the first triplet in the aC series, we again return to the regular lowercase step and continue until the aC series is completed. This will place the number aCb in cell [2,3,1], or what is the equivalent, in cell [2,0,1], and the number aCc in cell [3,1,1], or what is its equivalent, in cell [0,1,1]. Here you are blocked again and you will find that if you attempt to take another capital letter cross-step you will still be blocked, once again by the number aAa.

(7) It is evident that another special move (which we shall refer to as the *italic cross-step*) is necessary to start the bA series. This cross-step, which we shall identify as the (C+c+c, R+r+r, D+d+d) cross-step, consists of (C+c+c) columns to the right (left when (C+c+c) is negative), (R+r+r) rows up (down when (R+r+r) is negative), and (D+d+d) cells back (forward when (D+d+d) is negative). For Case 1, this consists of two cells to the right, two cells up, and two cells back. It follows that bAa belongs in cell [2,3,3], or what is its equivalent, in cell [2,0,0]. Figure 2–1 shows the situation at this point.

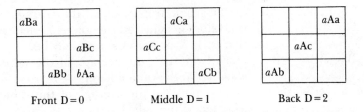

aBa		
		aBc
	aBb	bAa

Front D = 0

	aCa	
aCc		
		aCb

Middle D = 1

		aAa
	aAc	
aAb		

Back D = 2

FIGURE 2–1. THE a SERIES OF A THIRD-ORDER INTERMEDIATE CUBE

(8)   Repeat the above process until the cube is completely filled, as shown in Figure 2–2.

*a*Ba	*b*Ac	*c*Cb
*b*Ab	*c*Ca	*a*Bc
*c*Cc	*a*Bb	*b*Aa

Front D = 0

*c*Ab	*a*Ca	*b*Bc
*a*Cc	*b*Bb	*c*Aa
*b*Ba	*c*Ac	*a*Cb

Middle D = 1

*b*Cc	*c*Bb	*a*Aa
*c*Ba	*a*Ac	*b*Cb
*a*Ab	*b*Ca	*c*Bc

Back D = 2

FIGURE 2–2. THIRD-ORDER INTERMEDIATE MAGIC CUBE

Examination will show that every possible combination of three letters, consisting of one letter of each different type, appears once and only once. It follows that if we let

a, b, c equal in any order 0, 1, 2 or 0, 3, 6, or 0, 9, 18,
A, B, C equal in any order either of the above two series not selected for a, b, and c, and
a, b, c equal in any order the remaining series not selected for a, b, c, or for A, B, and C,

we shall find that, upon replacing the letters in each cell by the sum of the values assigned to them, the cube will consist of the numbers 0 to 26, as required.

Also, since the letters a, b, and c (and also A, B, and C and *a, b,* and *c*) appear once and only once in each orthogonal, the sum of the numbers in any given orthogonal will necessarily equal $0 + 1 + 2 + 0 + 3 + 6 + 0 + 9 + 18 = 39$, as required.

It is obvious that there is no way to assign these values so that the main diagonals of the orthogonal sections parallel to the faces of the cube will be magic. Let us therefore go on to the space diagonals.

*c*Cb   *b*Bb   *a*Ab   To be magic b must equal the average of the values assigned to the lowercase letters, that is, 1, 3, or 9, as the case may be.

*a*Ba   *b*Bb   *c*Bc   Here B must be the average of the values assigned to the capital letters.

*b*Aa   *b*Bb   *b*Cc   Here *b* must be the average of the values assigned to the italic letters.

*c*Cc   *b*Bb   *a*Aa   With no restrictions this diagonal is automatically magic.

We thus see that there are six ways to assign a value to a (from the first series, 0 or 2, 0 from the second series, 0 or 6, and from the third series, 0 or 18). For each of these six ways there is only one way left in the same series to assign values to b and c. Four ways still remain, however, to select a value for A (any one of the six values listed above after you eliminate the two chosen for the italic letters) and two ways remain to make a selection for a. This gives us a total of forty-eight ways $(6 \times 4 \times 2)$ that the available values can be assigned to the various letters and still get a magic cube consisting of the numbers 0 to 26, inclusive. Now by adding 1 to the number in each cell we have forty-eight normal magic cubes (each consisting of the numbers 1 to 27, inclusive) whose orthogonals and whose space diagonals add to 42. Not all of these cubes will be different in a magic sense; each is a rotation, reflection, or combination of rotations and reflections of some of the others.

Careful study will show that regardless of the values that you used to construct your cube, you will have four sets of cubes (of twelve cubes each), any one of which may be converted to any other one of the same set by simple rotation of the cube or by a combination of rotation and reflection (as in a mirror). Since a set of cubes with this property is considered to be only one basic cube, it follows that our forty-eight cubes reduce to four basic ones. These four sets are identical to the four basic cubes constructed by John B. Hendricks in connection with his proof that only four such cubes could exist (see Chapter 1). It follows that we can select any one of the cubes in each set as one of our four basic cubes, but in order to simplify our choice. let us use the italic letters in our intermediate cube to represent the "hundreds" digits, the capital letters to represent the "tens" digits, and the lowercase letters to represent the "units" digits. Thus if $a = 2$, C = 1, and a = 0, the number aCa will equal 210 to the base 3 (or $2N^2 + N + 0 = 21$ to base 10).

Hence let us set

1   $a = 0, b = 1, c = 2$; A = 0, B = 1, C = 2; and $a = 0, b = 1, c = 2$;
    or
2   $a = 2, b = 1, c = 0$; A = 0, B = 1, C = 2; and $a = 0, b = 1, c = 2$;
    or
3   $a = 0, b = 1, c = 2$; A = 2, B = 1, C = 0; and $a = 0, b = 1, c = 2$;
    or
4   $a = 2, b = 1, c = 0$; A = 2, B = 1, C = 0; and $a = 0, b = 1, c = 2$.

This will give us the four desired basic third-order magic cubes, each consisting of the numbers 0 to 26, as required.

Substituting these values for the letters in Figure 2–2 will give us Figure 2–3. Now all that remains to convert these four magic cubes to normal magic cubes consisting of the numbers 1 to 27, inclusive, with a magic constant of 42, is to convert to base 10 and add 1 to the number in each cell (see Figure 2–4).

Look at the three orthogonals through the center of each cube that are perpendicular to the faces of the cube. These are

Cube 1	9–14–19	7–14–21	3–14–25;
Cube 2	9–14–19	7–14–21	27–14–1;
Cube 3	9–14–19	3–14–25	27–14–1;
Cube 4	3–14–25	7–14–21	27–14–1.

Each of the four sets is different from the other three sets, thus it is not possible by any combinations of rotations and reflections to convert any one of these four cubes into any of the other three. This is why they are called basic cubes.

Cube 1	Cube 2	Cube 3	Cube 4

10	102	221
101	220	12
222	11	100

12	100	221
101	222	10
220	11	102

10	122	201
121	200	12
202	11	120

12	120	201
121	202	10
200	11	122

Front D = 0

201	20	112
22	111	200
110	202	21

201	22	110
20	111	202
112	200	21

221	0	112
2	111	220
110	222	1

221	2	110
0	111	222
112	220	1

Middle D = 1

122	211	0
210	2	121
1	120	212

120	211	2
212	0	121
1	122	210

102	211	20
210	22	101
21	100	212

100	211	22
212	20	101
21	102	210

Back D = 2

FIGURE 2–3. THIRD-ORDER MAGIC CUBES EXPRESSED TO BASE 3

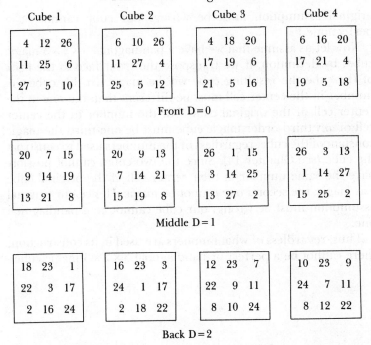

FIGURE 2–4. THIRD-ORDER MAGIC CUBES EXPRESSED TO BASE 10

Notice also how easy it is to check the magic properties of the orthogonals in Figure 2–3. The sum of the "hundreds" digits, the "tens" digits, and the "units" digits is 3 in each case.

While it is obvious that none of these four cubes are perfect or pandiagonal, the question still remains if it is possible for *any* $3 \times 3 \times 3$ magic cube, regardless of the numbers used in its construction, to be either perfect or pandiagonal. The answer is no. Assume that we have a perfect $3 \times 3 \times 3$ magic cube. The number in the center cell of a 3×3 magic square must equal one-third the magic constant of the square (see Chapter 14). By definition every orthogonal section parallel to one of the faces of a perfect cube must be a magic square with a magic constant equal to that of the cube itself. Each must therefore have in its center cell the number equal to one-third of the magic constant of the cube. This is impossible; all the orthogonal sections cannot have the same number in their center cell. Hence our original assumption must be wrong; our cube cannot be a perfect one.[1]

Now let us assume that we have a pandiagonal $3 \times 3 \times 3$ magic cube; by definition, if we transpose the front face to the back of the cube the resulting cube will be magic. In this cube the number in the center cell must be different than the one in the center cell of the original cube, but the number in the center cell of *any* third-order magic cube must be one-third the magic constant of the cube, regardless of the numbers used to construct the cube (see Chapter 14). Since the two cubes cannot possibly have the same number in their center cell, if the original cube was magic, the second one cannot be magic. Hence our original assumption must be wrong; our cube cannot be a pandiagonal one.

Thus, regardless of what numbers are used in its construction, there cannot be a perfect or pandiagonal $3 \times 3 \times 3$ magic cube.

1. This proof is a slight modification of one given by Richard Lewis Myers, Jr., that no *normal* magic cube of order 3 can exist (discussed in Martin Gardner, "Mathematical Games," *Scientific American* [January 1976], pp. 120, 122). See Chapter 14 for a detailed explanation.

Chapter 3

Fourth-Order Magic Cubes

It is relatively simple to extend the method for constructing doubly-even-order magic squares to doubly-even-order magic cubes. We shall demonstrate it by constructing a fourth-order magic cube.

Write the numbers 1 to 64, inclusive, in their natural order in a fourth-order cube (see Figure 3–1). All that is necessary to

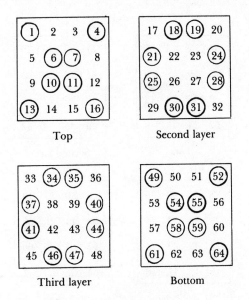

FIGURE 3–1. FOURTH-ORDER NATURAL CUBE

construct a doubly-even-order magic square (one where N is divisible by 4) is to write the numbers 1 to N^2 in their natural order in a blank $N \times N$ square and then to interchange numbers with their complements according to the rule that whenever you interchange a number (say one in column w and row x) with its complement (which happens to be in column y and row z), you also interchange the number in column w and row z with *its* complement (which you will find in column y and row x). Follow this rule until you have interchanged one-half of the numbers in each row and in each column. For a doubly-even-order cube the rule is that whenever you interchange a number (say the one in cell $[r,s,t]$) with its complement (in cell $[x,y,z]$), you also interchange the number in cell $[r,y,t]$ with its complement (which you will find in cell $[x,s,z]$); the number in cell $[x,s,t]$ with its complement (in cell $[r,y,z]$); and finally the number in cell $[x,y,t]$ with its complement (cell $[r,s,z]$). Remember that the sum of a number and its complement is twice the average value of the numbers forming the square or the cube, that is, their sum will be $(N^2 - 1)$ in the case of a square and $(N^3 - 1)$ in the case of a cube.

64	2	3	61
5	59	58	8
9	55	54	12
52	14	15	49

Top

17	47	46	20
44	22	23	41
40	26	27	37
29	35	34	32

Second layer

33	31	30	36
28	38	39	25
24	42	43	21
45	19	18	48

Third layer

16	50	51	13
53	11	10	56
57	7	6	60
4	62	63	1

Bottom

FIGURE 3–2. FOURTH-ORDER MAGIC CUBE

For a fourth-order cube all that is necessary is to interchange sets of eight symmetrically located numbers until you have interchanged one-half the numbers in each orthogonal. One way of doing this is by interchanging the numbers circled in Figure 3–1, each number being interchanged with its complement. Figure 3–2 shows the cube after the changes are made. Note that these interchanges correct the sums of the numbers in the orthogonals, but do not change the sums of the numbers in the space diagonals (which were correct in the original cube).

Now let us extend our knowledge of the cyclical method (combined with an intermediate letter cube), paying particular attention to the requirements to be met. In the last chapter we were particularly interested in generating the cube itself, and we shall follow the same method here, but since Δ equaled 2 in Case 1 and 2 is not prime to 4, it is necessary to select a new set of generating characteristics. As Case 2 we will consider

$$\begin{vmatrix} 1 & 2 & 2 \\ 2 & 1 & 2 \\ 2 & 2 & 1 \end{vmatrix}_N$$

where Δ equals -5.

In Case 1 we saw that the orthogonals were automatically magic. Could this have been predicted before constructing the cube? The answer is yes. As shown in Figure 3–3, the controlling characteristics for the orthogonals are the first minors of Δ. (See Chapter 13 for further discussion.) Substituting the values of

	x	X	x
Perpendicular to the side	$(rd - rd)$	$-(rD - Rd)$	$(rD - Rd)$
Perpendicular to the top	$-(cd - cd)$	$(cD - Cd)$	$-(cD - Cd)$
Perpendicular to the front	$(cr - cr)$	$-(cR - Cr)$	$(cR - Cr)$

FIGURE 3–3. CONTROLLING CHARACTERISTICS OF THE ORTHOGONALS

	x	X	x
Perpendicular to the side	$+1$	$+1$	-1
Perpendicular to the top	$+1$	-1	$+1$
Perpendicular to the front	-1	$+1$	$+1$

FIGURE 3–4. CONTROLLING CHARACTERISTICS OF THE ORTHOGONALS FOR CASE 1

the generating characteristics for Case 1 gives us Figure 3–4 and for Case 2 Figure 3–5.

Since for Case 1 all of the controlling characteristics and Δ are prime to any odd number, it follows that the orthogonals of any odd cube generated from Case 1's governing characteristics will have the same sum regardless of the values assigned to the various letters.

	x 3	X −2	x −2
Perpendicular to the side	3	−2	−2
Perpendicular to the top	−2	3	−2
Perpendicular to the front	−2	−2	3

FIGURE 3–5. CONTROLLING CHARACTERISTICS OF THE ORTHOGONALS FOR CASE 2

Looking at the values given in Figure 3–5, we can see that in Case 2 the controlling characteristics are not prime to N. On the other hand none of them equal 0 mod N. It follows that a fourth-order cube can be constructed ($\Delta = -5$ is prime to 4) and, since in some cases the controlling characteristic has a common factor with N, we must expect to find some duplication in the letters where this common factor occurs. We will show in Chapter 13 that where s is the greatest common divisor of the controlling characteristic and N, there will be N/s different letters, each appearing s times. Thus in Case 2 we predict that when the controlling characteristic is -2, there will be $4/2 = 2$ different letters, each appearing two times, and that when it is 3, there will be $4/1 = 4$ different letters, each appearing one time only.

We also prove in Chapter 13 that whenever N is odd, or whenever N is even and the number of different letters is also even, it is possible to assign values to those letters that will make the orthogonal in question magic. We therefore expect to be able to make all the orthogonals magic in a fourth-order cube constructed with the generating values of Case 2.

Let us now look at the controlling characteristics for the main diagonals of the orthogonal sections parallel to the various faces of the cube. (Remember that one of the requirements for a perfect cube is that all of these diagonals must be magic.) If the sum or difference of any pair of the three controlling characteristics for x, or for X and x (that is, the controlling characteristic for x in the orthogonals perpendicular to the side, for x in the orthogonals perpendicular to the top, and for x in the orthogonals perpendicular to the front), is 0 or a multiple of N, x will appear as a single letter in at least one of the sets of diagonals and it will not be possible to assign values to the letters for x so that all of the diagonals will have the correct sum. Since the difference of two equal numbers is always 0, we see from Figures 3–4 and 3–5 that these diagonals cannot be made correct for Cases 1 and 2.

How about the space diagonals? Here the controlling characteristics are obtained by taking all possible sums and differences of the three controlling characteristics for the orthogonals. For example, in Case 1 for x this becomes $1 \pm 1 \pm 1 \equiv -1$, 1, or 3. It follows that in our third-order cube we should expect to find x represented by a single letter in at least one of the space diagonals as, in fact, we did. In the case of the space diagonals, however, we were able to correct this by assigning the value 1 (the average value of 0, 1, 2, . . . , $(N-1)$) to this letter. Since the same situation exists for X and x, we should expect to find, as we did, the same situation in the case of these letters. In Case 2 the controlling characteristics for x (and, of course, for X and x also) becomes $3 \pm 2 \pm 2 \equiv -1$, 3, or 7. It follows that in every doubly-even-order cube constructed with the generating characteristics of Case 2 we expect to find that all space diagonals, both main and broken, are automatically correct (that is, we expect to find every letter appearing once, and only once, in every diagonal). In other words, we expect our fourth-order cube to be a pandiagonal magic cube.

Now let us construct our fourth-order intermediate cube and see if it meets our predictions. (It is the great flexibility of such cubes that gives the method its power.) It is constructed by following the method for a third-order magic cube without any change whatsoever (see Figure 3–6).

As expected, x in the orthogonals perpendicular to the side, X in the orthogonals perpendicular to the top, and x in the orthogonals perpendicular to the front consist of four different letters, each appearing once and only once. In all other cases the various letters appear in pairs, as expected.

It is also obvious that the main diagonals of the orthogonal sections cannot be made magic. A check will show that the space diagonals are pandiagonal.

cDc	aBd	cDa	aBb
aCa	cAb	aCc	cAd
cBc	aDd	cBa	aDb
aAa	cCb	aAc	cCd

Front D = 0

dBa	bDb	dBc	bDd
bAc	dCd	bAa	dCb
dDa	bBb	dDc	bBd
bCc	dAd	bCa	dAb

D = 1

aDc	cBd	aDa	cBb
cCa	aAb	cCc	aAd
aBc	cDd	aBa	cDb
cAa	aCb	cAc	aCd

D = 2

bBa	dDb	bBc	dDd
dAc	bCd	dAa	bCb
bDa	dBb	bDc	dBd
dCc	bAd	dCa	bAb

Back D = 3

FIGURE 3–6. INTERMEDIATE FOURTH-ORDER CUBE

22	313	21	310
331	0	332	3
12	323	11	320
301	30	302	33

Front D = 0

111	220	112	223
202	133	201	130
121	210	122	213
232	103	231	100

D = 1

322	13	321	10
31	300	32	303
312	23	311	20
1	330	2	333

D = 2

211	120	212	123
102	233	101	230
221	110	222	113
132	203	131	200

Back D = 3

FIGURE 3–7. PANDIAGONAL FOURTH-ORDER MAGIC CUBE EXPRESSED TO BASE 4

Since the letters are paired—A with C and B with D—it follows that we must select values that not only will result in the cube containing the numbers 0 to 63 but will also make $A + C = B + D$, $a + c = b + d$, and $a + c = b + d$. There are various ways that this can be done. One of them is: $A = 0$, $B = 1$, $C = 3$, $D = 2$, $a = 1$, $b = 0$, $c = 2$, $d = 3$, $a = 3$, $b = 2$, $c = 0$, and $d = 1$.

It is a simple matter to check Figure 3–7 to see that the sum of the orthogonals is correct, the sum for the italic, capital, and lowercase letters being 6 in every instance. In order to check the space diagonal properties, it is convenient to examine the two main diagonal planes—those perpendicular to the side and containing the main diagonals as well as the space diagonals (see Figure 3–8). Note that the diagonals, both main and broken, are correct in both of these squares. Similar results will be obtained if the diagonal planes are taken perpendicular to the front or to the top of the cube. Thus, as predicted, the space diagonals are pandiagonal.

22	313	21	310		301	30	302	33
202	133	201	130		121	210	122	213
312	23	311	20		31	300	32	303
132	203	131	200		211	120	212	123

Plane passing through the   Plane passing through the
upper front and lower   lower front and upper
back orthogonals   back orthogonals

FIGURE 3–8. TWO MAIN DIAGONAL PLANES

It remains only to convert Figure 3–7 to base 10 and to add 1 to the number in each cell to obtain Figure 3–9, the predicted pandiagonal fourth-order magic cube. The reader may have observed that in both this case and that of the third-order magic cube constructed in Chapter 2 we constructed the orthogonal sections parallel to the front of the cube. How about the orthogonal sections parallel to the side and those parallel to the top? We could give generating characteristics for these cubes that would result in these sections, but that would be the hard way; it is much easier to construct them directly from Figure

				Row				
11	56	10	53	3	22	41	23	44
62	1	63	4	2	35	32	34	29
7	60	6	57	1	26	37	27	40
50	13	51	16	0	47	20	46	17

Column   0 1 2 3   0 1 2 3

Front section D = 0   Second section D = 1

59	8	58	5	3	38	25	39	28
14	49	15	52	2	19	48	18	45
55	12	54	9	1	42	21	43	24
2	61	3	64	0	31	36	30	33

Column   0 1 2 3   0 1 2 3

Third section D = 2   Back section D = 3

FIGURE 3–9. PANDIAGONAL FOURTH-ORDER MAGIC CUBE

				Depth				
38	25	39	28	3	19	48	18	45
59	8	58	5	2	14	49	15	52
22	41	23	44	1	35	32	34	29
11	56	10	53	0	62	1	63	4

Column   0 1 2 3   0 1 2 3

Top section R = 3   Second section R = 2

42	21	43	24	3	31	36	30	33
55	12	54	9	2	2	61	3	64
26	37	27	40	1	47	20	46	17
7	60	6	57	0	50	13	51	16

Column   0 1 2 3   0 1 2 3

Third section R = 1   Bottom section R = 0

FIGURE 3–10. ANOTHER VIEW OF A PANDIAGONAL CUBE

3–9. Notice that in Figure 3–9 we have indicated the number of the row, column, and depth of each cell. The four orthogonals labeled Row 3 form the top orthogonal section, those labeled Row 2 form the next section, and so on (see Figure 3–10). The four orthogonals labeled Column 0 form the left orthogonal section, those labeled Column 1 form the next-to-left section, and so on (see Figure 3–11). We now have all twelve of the orthogonal sections of our fourth-order pandiagonal magic cube.

				Row				
38	59	22	11	3	25	8	41	56
19	14	35	62	2	48	49	32	1
42	55	26	7	1	21	12	37	60
31	2	47	50	0	36	61	20	13

Depth   3 2 1 0   3 2 1 0

Left section C = 0   Next-to-left section C = 1

39	58	23	10	3	28	5	44	53
18	15	34	63	2	45	52	29	4
43	54	27	6	1	24	9	40	57
30	3	46	51	0	33	64	17	16

Depth   3 2 1 0   3 2 1 0

Next-to-right section C = 2   Right section C = 3

FIGURE 3–11. A THIRD VIEW OF A PANDIAGONAL CUBE

Having constructed a fourth-order pandiagonal magic cube, how about a fourth-order perfect magic cube? None exists. Richard Schroeppel proved this in 1972. Essentially his proof is as follows.

Note that if a cube is a perfect magic cube, all orthogonal sections parallel to any face of the cube, and all diagonal sections perpendicular to any of the faces, are magic squares. The first step is to show that for any fourth-order magic square the sum of the four corners equals the magic constant, say K. Now label the sixteen cells forming such a square (see Figure 3–12). Examination of Figure 3–12 shows that

$$A + B + C + D = K$$
$$A + E + I + M = K$$
$$A + F + K + P = K$$
$$D + G + J + M = K$$
$$D + H + L + P = K$$
$$M + N + O + P = K$$

If we add these six equations together and subtract the letters A to P, inclusive (whose sum equals 4K), we have left

$$2A + 2D + 2M + 2P = 2K$$

which reduces to

$$A + D + M + P = K,$$

our first lemma.

A	B	C	D
E	F	G	H
I	J	K	L
M	N	O	P

FIGURE 3–12. A STEP TOWARD SCHROEPPEL'S PROOF

Now consider the cube's eight corners. Let us label them as in Figure 3–13.

From the top section we have $\qquad A + B + C + D = K$
From the front section we have $\qquad A + B + E + F = K$
From the diagonal section perpendicular side $C + D + E + F = K$

If we subtract the last of these three equations from the sum of the first two we get

$$2A + 2B = K$$

or

$$A + B = K/2,$$

our second lemma; any two corners lying on the same orthogonal of a fourth-order perfect magic cube have a sum equal to $K/2$. Now consider corner B. It is connected to A, D, and F. Therefore, according to lemma 2,

$$A + B = D + B = F + B = K/2$$

If we subtract B from each equality we have

$$A = D = F,$$

which is clearly impossible. It follows that our original assumption—that the cube was a perfect one—is incorrect. Therefore it is not possible for a perfect fourth-order magic cube to exist.[1]

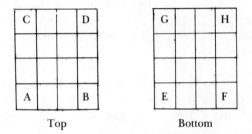

Top   Bottom

FIGURE 3–13. SCHROEPPEL'S PROOF: THE CORNERS OF THE CUBE

1. Michael Beeler, William Gosper, and Richard Schroeppel, "Artificial Intelligence Memo No. 239," Massachusetts Institute of Technology, Artificial Intelligence Laboratory (February 29, 1977), items 50–51.

Chapter 4

Fifth-Order Magic Cubes

The cube we have designated Case 1 provides all we need to construct a pandiagonal fifth-order magic cube. As in Chapters 2 and 3, the controlling characteristics are for Δ, 2; for the orthogonals, -1 and $+1$; and for the space diagonals, -1, $+1$, and $+3$. Since all of these values are prime to 5, we expect no difficulty.

It remains only to follow the rule given in Chapter 2 for the construction of the cube to arrive at Figure 4–1. Also, since our end product will be pandiagonal, it makes no difference in what cell we place the number aAa. Let us place it in cell [0,0,0] as a matter of convenience.

Examination of Figure 4–1 shows that, as expected, each different letter appears once and only once in each of the orthogonals and in each space diagonal. It follows that if we assign the values 0, 1, 2, 3, and 4 to each set of italic, capital, and lowercase letters, we will generate a pandiagonal magic cube of the fifth order.

Clearly there are many different cubes that can be generated from this one intermediate cube. There are 120 different ways $(5 \times 4 \times 3 \times 2 \times 1)$ to assign the values to the italic letters. For each italic value there are 120 different ways to assign values to the capital letters. For each of these 14,400 (120×120) different ways there are 120 different ways to assign values to the lowercase letters—1,728,000 different ways in all. When we divide this number by 2 to eliminate complementary cubes, we still have 864,000 different pandiagonal fifth-order magic cubes. Of these, only those where $b=2$, $B=2$, $b=2$, and

$a+c=A+C=a+c=d+e=D+E=d+e=4$ will be symmetrical (that is, where the numbers in symmetrically located cells are complementary—have a sum equal to $(N-1)$). There are $8 \times 8 \times 8 \div 2 = 256$ such cubes.

Needless to say, these cubes will consist of the numbers 0 to 124, inclusive. It will be necessary to add 1 to the number in

cDc	eBa	bEd	dCb	aAe
eBe	bEc	dCa	aAd	cDb
bEb	dCe	aAc	cDa	eBd
dCd	aAb	cDe	eBc	bEa
aAa	cDd	eBb	bEe	dCc

Front D = 0

aBe	cEc	eCa	bAd	dDb
cEb	eCe	bAc	dDa	aBd
eCd	bAb	dDe	aBc	cEa
bAa	dDd	aBb	cEe	eCc
dDc	aBa	cEd	eCb	bAe

D = 1

dEb	aCe	cAc	eDa	bBd
aCd	cAb	eDe	bBc	dEa
cAa	eDd	bBb	dEe	aCc
eDc	bBa	dEd	aCb	cAe
bBe	dEc	aCa	cAd	eDb

D = 2

bCd	dAb	aDe	cBc	eEa
dAa	aDd	cBb	eEe	bCc
aDc	cBa	eEd	bCb	dAe
cBe	eEc	bCa	dAd	aDb
eEb	bCe	dAc	aDa	cBd

D = 3

eAa	bDd	dBb	aEe	cCc
bDc	dBa	aEd	cCb	eAe
dBe	aEc	cCa	eAd	bDb
aEb	cCe	eAc	bDa	dBd
cCd	eAb	bDe	dBc	aEa

Back D = 4

FIGURE 4–1. PANDIAGONAL FIFTH-ORDER MAGIC CUBE

each cell to convert each cube to a normal one consisting of the numbers 1 to 125, inclusive. Let us set $a = A = a = 0$, $b = B = b = 2$, $c = C = c = 4$, $d = D = d = 1$, and $e = E = e = 3$. Substituting these values in Figure 4–1 will generate Figure 4–2.

Notice that, as predicted, the "hundreds," "tens," and "units" of all orthogonals consist of 0, 1, 2, 3, and 4. Hence the

414	320	231	142	3
323	234	140	1	412
232	143	4	410	321
141	2	413	324	230
0	411	322	233	144

Front D = 0

23	434	340	201	112
432	343	204	110	21
341	202	113	24	430
200	111	22	433	344
114	20	431	342	203

D = 1

132	43	404	310	221
41	402	313	224	130
400	311	222	133	44
314	220	131	42	403
223	134	40	401	312

D = 2

241	102	13	424	330
100	11	422	333	244
14	420	331	242	103
423	334	240	101	12
332	243	104	10	421

D = 3

300	211	122	33	444
214	120	31	442	303
123	34	440	301	212
32	443	304	210	121
441	302	213	124	30

Back D = 4

FIGURE 4–2. SYMMETRICAL PANDIAGONAL FIFTH-ORDER MAGIC CUBE TO BASE 5

orthogonals of the final cube must be magic. Now, as we did for the fourth-order cube, let us construct the two diagonal sections perpendicular to the left face (see Figure 4–3).

414	320	231	142	3
432	343	204	110	21
400	311	222	133	44
423	334	240	101	12
441	302	213	124	30

0	411	322	233	144
200	111	22	433	344
400	311	222	133	44
100	11	422	333	244
300	211	122	33	444

FIGURE 4–3. DIAGONAL SECTIONS

Notice that, as predicted, all diagonals in both sections, both main and broken, are also automatically correct. We would have obtained similar results if the diagonal sections had been taken perpendicular to the front or the top of the cube. As expected, the cube is pandiagonal. It is a simple matter to convert to base 10 and add 1 to the number in each cell (see Figure 4–4).

There is no question as to whether or not pandiagonal fifth-order magic cubes exist—we have just constructed one. But how about perfect fifth-order cubes? It is believed that they do not exist, but as far as we can determine, no proof exists. The only way we know to settle the question would be to present it to a large computer, but we can eliminate some possibilities.

Lemma 1. It is impossible to construct a perfect fifth-order magic cube by using cyclical three-dimension vectors such as those we employed to make the pandiagonal cube.

As stated in the last chapter (and proven in Chapter 13) there are controlling characteristics (based on the values given to C, R, D, c, r, d, c, r, and d) for the orthogonals. These characteristics have certain properties, namely:

(a) They cannot equal zero. If they did it would not be possible to assign values to the generating characteristics that would make all the orthogonals correct.
(b) They must be less than 5. Any larger than 5 would be reduced to some number less than 5 since we are dealing with

110	86	67	48	4
89	70	46	2	108
68	49	5	106	87
47	3	109	90	66
1	107	88	69	50

Front D = 0

14	120	96	52	33
118	99	55	31	12
97	53	34	15	116
51	32	13	119	100
35	11	117	98	54

D = 1

43	24	105	81	62
22	103	84	65	41
101	82	63	44	25
85	61	42	23	104
64	45	21	102	83

D = 2

72	28	9	115	91
26	7	113	94	75
10	111	92	73	29
114	95	71	27	8
93	74	30	6	112

D = 3

76	57	38	19	125
60	36	17	123	79
39	20	121	77	58
18	124	80	56	37
122	78	59	40	16

Back D = 4

FIGURE 4–4. SYMMETRICAL PANDIAGONAL FIFTH-ORDER MAGIC CUBE TO BASE 10

cyclical operations where $(x + 5k)$ is equivalent to x.

(c) If the sum or difference of any two of the three controlling characteristics for x—or for X or x—is 0 or a multiple of N (that is, if any pair of the controlling characteristics for x in the orthogonals perpendicular to the side, in the orthogonals perpendicular to the top, or in the orthogonals perpendicular to the front has a sum or difference equal to 0 or a multiple of N), x will appear as a single letter in at least one of the sets of diagonals of the orthogonal sections. Thus it will be impossible to assign values to the lowercase letters in the intermediate square to make the diagonals all magic (which is a requirement for a perfect magic cube).

From (a) and (b) above it follows that the controlling characteristics must be 1, 2, 3, or 4. From (c) above we see that no two of the three characteristics for x (or X or x) can be alike. Therefore these three characteristics can only be 1, 2, and 3, or 1, 2, and 4, or 2, 3, and 4. But in each of these three combinations two of the characteristics add to 5. It follows that no possible selection of generating characteristics can generate a set of controlling characteristics that will make it possible to construct a perfect fifth-order magic cube. This proves Lemma 1.

Chapter 5

The First Perfect Magic Cube

Now let us turn to Dr. Barnard's article, which we mentioned in Chapter 1. The article is remarkable for its thoroughness, especially when you consider that it was published in 1888. We reprint here a brief excerpt from it and run into it a lengthy footnote to the article that is of interest to us at the moment. Dr. Barnard begins by describing the circumstances under which he first heard of this $8 \times 8 \times 8$ perfect magic cube—the first such cube known to appear in print. He goes on to give instructions for constructing a sixteenth-order cube, but in the interest of saving space—and, we hope, of reconstructing the original eighth-order cube—we illustrate his method by constructing an eighth-order cube.

> The arrangement of the terms of an arithmetical series in the form of a cube, so that each linear row of terms parallel to the edges, or to the diagonals, may sum up equally, is a problem which appears not to have been hitherto considered.
>
> . . . .
>
> This statement, though true so far as the knowledge of the writer extended at the time it was written, may possibly not be strictly correct. At a period somewhat later there was received by post from an unknown source a printed leaflet containing a magic cube of the number 8, accompanied by a geometric diagram, to which the somewhat fanciful name of "magic reciprocals" was given, but the meaning of which was not intelligible. This was probably the first example of a magic cube put into print. In a letter

addressed by its author, early in 1876, to Prof. P. H. Wanderweyde, editor of the *Manufacturer and Builder,* New York, and published in that periodical, it is stated that the publication of this magic cube was first made in the *Commercial,* a daily paper of Cincinnati, and that it appeared on the 11th of March, 1875. This, of course, antedates any similar publication from any other source; but it does not solve the question who first constructed a magic cube, since the theory given in the text of the present article was perfected long before its presentation to the Academy, which took place in June, 1875. This is no impeachment of the originality of the inventor of this magic cube of 8, Prof. Gustavus Frankenstein, now [1888] resident in Springfield, Ohio.

The example as published was unaccompanied by any statement of the method of construction, or any demonstration of the truth of its theory. In what manner it was actually constructed, therefore, it is impossible to say; but by a scrutiny of the example itself it is not difficult to detect a method by which, whether that of the author or not, the result may be obtained. That method may be explained as follows.

Let the root number of the cube be represented by N. Take a square of N^2 vacant cells. Beginning in the upper horizontal row at the left-hand cell with unity, write the numbers of the first linear grade in their order from left to right; only omit the even terms, leaving their cells vacant, until the central axis is reached; and after passing the axis omit the odd terms and write the even terms only in the cells which belong to them. The extreme term then on the right will be N, as that on the left was 1. In the next horizontal row below write, in exactly like manner, the terms of the second linear grade, and pursue this course until the number of grades written is equal to $N/4$. In the next horizontal row below write the terms of the next following linear grade, which will be $N/4+1$; only now omit the odd terms on the left of the axis and insert the even terms only in their proper places; while on the right of the axis are to be omitted the even terms and the odd terms are to be written; and this rule is to be followed in the several successive grades until the $3N/4$ grade has been written. After that let the remaining grades be written, according to the law observed in the grades first written, when the last term in the lower right-hand corner will be N^2.

Take, now, a second square entirely similar to the first, and write in it the successive linear grades in the same manner as in the first, except in the particulars following: The first linear grade is to be written in the lowermost instead of the uppermost row, and the order must be from the right to the left instead of from left to right, the odd numbers being omitted and the even numbers written on the right of the axis, while on the left the odd numbers are to be written and the even numbers omitted. The successive grades are then to follow each other in the successive rows upward, and the terms are to be inscribed in the same law as in the first until the $N/4$ grade has been reached. After that the odd numbers are to be written and the even numbers omitted on the right, while on the left the even numbers are to be written and the odd numbers omitted until the $3N/4$ grade has been entered, after which the remaining grades are to follow the law observed in the first. It will then be seen that in these two squares are contained all of the terms from 1 to N^2, that is to say, all the terms of the first quadrate grade the terms omitted in the first being produced in the second and *vice versa*. To complete these squares as elements in the cube the blanks must be filled with the complements of the terms omitted, that is to say, with the differences between the omitted terms and the sum of the extremes, which is $N^3 + 1$. These complements will be the consequents in the couplets formed as in Section VIII, and it will be seen that each such complement is situated precisely symmetrically opposite to its antecedent in the other square.

With all the blanks thus filled these two squares will be the first and last of the proposed cube [see Figure 5–1]. Another pair of squares similar to these are next to be filled with the terms of the second quadrate grade, following precisely the same law as the first two for all of numbers greater than 8, but for the cube of 8 the second pair of squares must reverse the law of the first in regard to the positions of the odd and even terms relative to the vertical axis. This pair of squares being completed [see Figure 5–2], a third pair is to be filled with the terms of the third quadrate grade, following the law of the second in regard to the position of the odd and even terms [see Figure 5–3]. A fourth pair is then to be filled with the terms of the fourth quadrate grade, following the law of the first pair [see Figure 5–4].

The blank squares being filled in all these squares the cube is complete, and it only remains to arrange them in their proper order. Thus, the first pair furnish the first and eighth of the cube, the second pair furnish the second and seventh, the third pair furnish the third and sixth, and the fourth pair the fourth and fifth.

For an even number greater than 8 the law of the first pair given above is to be followed in the second pair also, and likewise in the third and fourth until the number of pairs equals $N/8$ or the number of single squares equals $N/4$. After that the law of the second pair of the cube of 8 is to be followed until the number of pairs equal to $3N/8$ has been completed, or $3N/4$ single squares. The remaining pairs are then to follow the law of the first.

. . . .

The magic character of the cube may be proved as follows: First, for the horizontal rows. From the law of construction it is obvious that each horizontal row contains a number of terms equal to $N/2$; also that these terms are severally situated symmetrically to each other relatively to the central axis. The sum of each such symmetrically situated pair of terms is equal, by the laws of arithmetical series, to the sum of the extremes, and the number of such pairs will be equal to $N/4$. In the upper row of the first square, therefore, the sum of all the terms will be equal $N(N+1)/4$. In the lower row of the second square will be the $N/2$ terms of the first linear grade, which were omitted in the upper row of the first square, and they will also be symmetrically situated to each other in pairs relatively to the central axis, and hence their sum will also be equal to $N(N+1)/4$. Now as the sums of these sets of antecedents are respectively equal, the sums of their consequents must also be equal, and hence, when these consequents are written in, the sum of either complete row must be equal to the sum of all of the terms of a number of couplets equal to $N/2$. The sum of each couplet is equal to the sum of the extremes of the cubic series, that is, to $N^3 + 1$; hence the sum of all the terms in the upper row of the first square or the lower row of the second square will be $N(N^3 + 1)/2$, which is the common sum of every separate row or column in the magic cube of N. The same demonstration applies to every pair of rows symmetrically situated, one in the first of the elementary squares, and the other in the last.

And the same is further applicable to the several rows in all the successive pairs of squares filled as above described.

For the vertical columns, it is obvious that, in the first square filled, we have a series of terms of which the first is unity and the common difference is N. Of the terms of this series we have the first one-fourth and the last one-fourth of the number in the first square on the left, the middle two-fourths being in the second on the right. By the properties of arithmetical series it follows that the sum of the antecedents on one side is equal to the sum of those on the other. Hence, when their consequents are written in, the sums of the entire columns will be equal, and, as before, will be severally expressible by $N(N^3 + 1)/2$. For the rows in the third direction, that is to say, at right angles to the planes of the squares, it is evident that, beginning at the upper left-hand corner of the first square we have a series of which the first term is 1 and the common difference is N^2, half of the terms of which are in one square on the left and half in the other on the right, being situated to each other in pairs symmetrically to the middle point. The sums of these terms are therefore severally equal, and when their consequents are written in the completed rows will be equal. These modes of explanation are applicable to all other rows parallel to either the vertical axis or to the axis perpendicular to the plane.

The diagonal rows will also be equal, for in the first square for example, the direct diagonal, if there had been no cells left vacant, would have been filled with a series of which the first term is 1 and the common difference is $N + 1$. The last term we have seen to be N^2, so that the sum of the extremes is $N^2 + 1$ and the sum of the series $N(N^2 + 1)/2$. A little consideration will show that, owing to the omission of terms during inscription, the number of terms actually written is only $N/2$, and that these terms are situated symmetrically to each other relatively to the middle point; hence, their sum will be only $N(N^2 + 1)/4$. If we take the transverse axis, we shall have a series of which the first term is N and the common difference is $N - 1$; hence, the last term is $N + (N - 1)(N - 1) = N^2 - N + 1$; and hence the sum of the extremes will be $N^2 + 1$, as in the former case; and in like manner the sum of all terms actually written in this diagonal will be $N(N^2 + 1)/4$ as before. Consequently, when the consequents are written in, these diagonal rows will once more be equal to each other and each equal the common sum $N(N^3 + 1)/2$.

As to the diagonals of the solid (what we shall later refer to as the space diagonals), it will easily appear that they must sum up equally, for every antecedent throughout the cube has its consequent symmetrically situated opposite to it relatively to the central point of the cube; hence, every solid diagonal contains both terms of as many couplets as is equal to $N/2$, and the sum of all the terms of such a diagonal is, therefore, $N(N^3 + 1)/2$.[1]

In order to round out the picture presented by Figures 5–1, 5–2, 5–3, and 5–4 (which show all the orthogonal sections

1	777	3	775	774	6	772	8
11	767	13	765	764	16	762	18
758	22	756	24	25	753	27	751
748	32	746	34	35	743	37	741
738	42	736	44	45	733	47	731
728	52	726	54	55	723	57	721
61	717	63	715	714	66	712	68
71	707	73	705	704	76	702	78

First square   Front D = 0

701	77	703	75	74	706	72	708
711	67	713	65	64	716	62	718
58	722	56	724	725	53	727	51
48	732	46	734	735	43	737	41
38	742	36	744	745	33	747	31
28	752	26	754	755	23	757	21
761	17	763	15	14	766	12	768
771	7	773	5	4	776	2	778

Second square   Back D = 7

FIGURE 5–1. CONSTRUCTING A PERFECT EIGHTH-ORDER CUBE

1. F. A. P. Barnard, "Theory of Magic Squares and of Magic Cubes," in *The Memoirs of the National Academy of Science* 4 (1888):209, 244–248.

parallel to the front of the eighth-order magic cube), we shall construct from them Figure 5–5 (the left side of the cube), Figure 5–6 (the top of the cube), and Figure 5–7 (the two diagonal sections perpendicular to the left side of the cube, which show the space diagonals).

Examination of these figures, which are to the base 8 (in every orthogonal, every main diagonal in the orthogonal sections, and every space diagonal, the sum of the "hundreds" and "tens" digits is 28 and the sum of the "units" digits is 36, as required), will show that they prove conclusively what Barnard claimed, namely, that the cube was a perfect eighth-order magic cube—and it was published over 100 years ago.

678	102	676	104	105	673	107	671
668	112	666	114	115	663	117	661
121	657	123	655	654	126	652	128
131	647	133	645	644	136	642	138
141	637	143	635	634	146	632	148
151	627	153	625	624	156	622	158
618	162	616	164	165	613	167	611
608	172	606	174	175	603	177	601

Third square   D = 1

178	602	176	604	605	173	607	171
168	612	166	614	615	163	617	161
621	157	623	155	154	626	152	628
631	147	633	145	144	636	142	638
641	137	643	135	134	646	132	648
651	127	653	125	124	656	122	658
118	662	116	664	665	113	667	111
108	672	106	674	675	103	677	101

Fourth square   D = 6

FIGURE 5–2. A FURTHER STEP TOWARD A PERFECT CUBE

578	202	576	204	205	573	207	571
568	212	566	214	215	563	217	561
221	557	223	555	554	226	552	228
231	547	233	545	544	236	542	238
241	537	243	535	534	246	532	248
251	527	253	525	524	256	522	258
518	262	516	264	265	513	267	511
508	272	506	274	275	503	277	501

Fifth square   D = 2

278	502	276	504	505	273	507	271
268	512	266	514	515	263	517	261
521	257	523	255	254	526	252	528
531	247	533	245	244	536	242	538
541	237	543	235	234	546	232	548
551	227	553	225	224	556	222	558
218	562	216	564	565	213	567	211
208	572	206	574	575	203	577	201

Sixth square   D = 5

FIGURE 5–3. THE THIRD STEP

301	477	303	475	474	306	472	308
311	467	313	465	464	316	462	318
458	322	456	324	325	453	327	451
448	332	446	334	335	443	337	441
438	342	436	344	345	433	347	431
428	352	426	354	355	423	357	421
361	417	363	415	414	366	412	368
371	407	373	405	404	376	402	378

Seventh square   D = 3

401	377	403	375	374	406	372	408
411	367	413	365	364	416	362	418
358	422	356	424	425	353	427	351
348	432	346	434	435	343	437	341
338	442	336	444	445	333	447	331
328	452	326	454	455	323	457	321
461	317	463	315	314	466	312	468
471	307	473	305	304	476	302	478

Eighth square   D = 4

FIGURE 5–4. THE FINAL STEP

701	77	703	75	74	706	72	708
178	602	176	604	605	173	607	171
278	502	276	504	505	273	507	271
401	377	403	375	374	406	372	408
301	477	303	475	474	306	472	308
578	202	576	204	205	573	207	571
678	102	676	104	105	673	107	671
1	777	3	775	774	6	772	8

Top   R = 7

FIGURE 5–5. A PERFECT CUBE FROM ABOVE

701	178	278	401	301	578	678	1
711	168	268	411	311	568	668	11
58	621	521	358	458	221	121	758
48	631	531	348	448	231	131	748
38	641	541	338	438	241	141	738
28	651	551	328	428	251	151	728
761	118	218	461	361	518	618	61
771	108	208	471	371	508	608	71

Left side   C = 0

FIGURE 5–6. SIDE VIEW OF A PERFECT CUBE

71	707	73	705	704	76	702	78
618	162	616	164	165	613	167	611
251	527	253	525	524	256	522	258
438	342	436	344	345	433	347	431
348	432	346	434	435	343	437	341
521	257	523	255	254	526	252	528
168	612	166	614	615	163	617	161
701	77	703	75	74	706	72	708

771	7	773	5	4	776	2	778
118	662	116	664	665	113	667	111
551	227	553	225	224	556	222	558
338	442	336	444	445	333	447	331
448	332	446	334	335	443	337	441
221	557	223	555	554	226	552	228
668	112	666	114	115	663	117	661
1	777	3	775	774	6	772	8

FIGURE 5–7. DIAGONAL SECTIONS PERPENDICULAR TO THE LEFT SIDE

Chapter 6

Triply-Even Magic Cubes

For convenience the construction of triply-even magic cubes (those where N is a multiple of 8) will be demonstrated by constructing eighth-order magic cubes. There is no loss in generality in so doing since, once the basic method is understood, it is a simple matter to extend it to higher order cubes such as 16, 24, and so on.

As far as the construction of simple magic cubes is concerned, we have covered the process in Chapter 3 in the constructing of fourth-order magic cubes. We started there with a natural-order cube using the numbers 1 to 64, inclusive; we shall start here with a similar cube using the numbers 1 to 512, inclusive, placing the numbers 1 to 64 in their natural order in the top ($R = 7$) layer, 65 to 128 in the next ($R = 6$) layer, and so on until you reach the bottom layer, which will consist of the numbers 449 to 512, inclusive.

We repeat here the general rule that governs our interchanges:

(1) Whenever you interchange a number (say one in cell $[r,s,t]$ with its complement in cell $[x,y,z]$) you also interchange the number in cell $[r,y,t]$ with its complement (which you will find in cell $[x,s,z]$); the number in cell $[x,s,t]$ with its complement (which you will find in cell $[r,y,z]$); and finally the number in cell $[x,y,t]$ with its complement (in cell $[r,s,z]$).

(2) Continue the interchanging of sets of eight symmetrically located numbers (as specified in (1) above) until you have interchanged one-half the numbers in each orthogonal.

If all you wish to do is to construct an eighth-order magic cube, you can stop here and any cube that you construct will meet the necessary requirements; if you want to construct an eighth-order *perfect* magic cube, there are additional requirements to be met.

(3)   Arrange the interchanges to be made on the top (and, of course, the bottom) layer so that one-half of the numbers in the horizontal and vertical orthogonals are interchanged, as are one-half of the numbers in the two main diagonals. These interchanges are shown in Figure 6–1, where the subscripts

X_1		X_2			X_2		X_1
	X_3		X_4	X_4		X_3	
	X_5		X_6	X_6		X_5	
X_7		X_8			X_8		X_7
X_7		X_8			X_8		X_7
	X_5		X_6	X_6		X_5	
	X_3		X_4	X_4		X_3	
X_1		X_2			X_2		X_1

FIGURE 6–1. CONSTRUCTING AN EIGHTH-ORDER CUBE

	X_{11}		X_{12}	X_{12}		X_{11}	
X_{13}		X_{14}			X_{14}		X_{13}
X_{15}		X_{16}			X_{16}		X_{15}
	X_{17}		X_{18}	X_{18}		X_{17}	
	X_{17}		X_{18}	X_{18}		X_{17}	
X_{15}		X_{16}			X_{16}		X_{15}
X_{13}		X_{14}			X_{14}		X_{13}
	X_{11}		X_{12}	X_{12}		X_{11}	

FIGURE 6–2. A CONVERSE LAYOUT

indicate the cells involved in the simultaneous interchanges. Figure 6–1 also applies to the bottom layer.

(4) It would be difficult to make similar layouts for the interchanges between the other pairs of layers of the cube. Therefore let us adopt the idea of using either Figure 6–1 or its converse, which is a similar layout with every blank cell in Figure 6–1 replaced by a transfer and vice versa (see Figure 6–2). Now all of the sections parallel to the top will consist of a magic square, thus meeting the requirements for a perfect magic cube. Further, in order to ensure that all of the orthogonals perpendicular to the top are magic, all that is necessary is to use the square shown in Figure 6–1 for one-half of the orthogonal sections parallel to the top and the one in Figure 6–2 for the remaining sections.

(5) Now it remains to see whether by adjusting the order in which you apply Figures 6–1 and 6–2 to the various layers of the cube, or by going back and adjusting Figures 6–1 and 6–2 themselves, you can have the diagonals in the front and side views be magic. For the front views, these layers will repeat the horizontal orthogonals of Figure 6–1 or the reverse thereof when you are using Figure 6–2. The side views repeat the vertical orthogonals.

It is not easy to meet the fifth requirement. We arrived at Figures 6–1 and 6–2 only after many trials and errors. If you use Figure 6–1 for the orthogonal sections R = 0, R = 1, R = 6, and R = 7 and Figure 6–2 for the remaining sections, Figure 6–3 will show the front view and Figure 6–4 the left side view. Both of these figures will generate magic squares. It follows that the cube we generate following this procedure will be a perfect eighth-order magic cube. See Figure 6–5 for the cube to the base 8 for ease in checking the magical properties of the orthogonals and main diagonals in the sections parallel to the top of the cube; Figure 6–6 for the same check in the front of the cube; Figure 6–7 for the same check in the left side of the cube; and Figure 6–8 for the diagonal sections perpendicular to the left side of the cube (for ease in checking the space diagonals). We use X to indicate transfers between R = 0 and R = 7; Y between R = 1 and R = 6; Z between R = 2 and R = 5; and W between R = 3 and R = 4.

X_1	X_2			X_2		X_1
Y_1	Y_2			Y_2		Y_1
	Z_{11}		Z_{12}	Z_{12}	Z_{11}	
	W_{11}		W_{12}	W_{12}	W_{11}	
	W_{11}		W_{12}	W_{12}	W_{11}	
	Z_{11}		Z_{12}	Z_{12}	Z_{11}	
Y_1	Y_2			Y_1		Y_2
X_1	X_2			X_2		X_1

FIGURE 6–3. FRONT VIEW

X_1			X_7	X_7			X_1
Y_1			Y_7	Y_7			Y_1
	Z_{13}	Z_{15}			Z_{15}	Z_{13}	
	W_{13}	W_{15}			W_{15}	W_{13}	
	W_{13}	W_{15}			W_{15}	W_{13}	
	Z_{13}	Z_{15}			Z_{15}	Z_{13}	
Y_1			Y_7	Y_7			Y_1
X_1			X_7	X_7			X_1

FIGURE 6–4. LEFT SIDE VIEW

777	1	775	3	4	772	6	770
10	766	12	764	763	15	761	17
20	756	22	754	753	25	751	27
747	31	745	33	34	742	36	740
737	41	735	43	44	732	46	730
50	726	52	724	723	55	721	57
60	716	62	714	713	65	711	67
707	71	705	73	74	702	76	700

$R = 7$

677	101	675	103	104	672	106	670
110	666	112	664	663	115	661	117
120	656	122	654	653	125	651	127
647	131	645	133	134	642	136	640
637	141	635	143	144	632	146	630
150	626	152	624	623	155	621	157
160	616	162	614	613	165	611	167
607	171	605	173	174	602	176	600

$R = 6$

200	576	202	574	573	205	571	207
567	211	565	213	214	562	216	560
557	221	555	223	224	552	226	550
230	546	232	544	543	235	541	237
240	536	242	534	533	245	531	247
527	251	525	253	254	522	256	520
517	261	515	263	264	512	266	510
270	506	272	504	503	275	501	277

$R = 5$

FIGURE 6–5 CONTINUED

300	476	302	474	473	305	471	307
467	311	465	313	314	462	316	460
457	321	455	323	324	452	326	450
330	446	332	444	443	335	441	337
340	436	342	434	433	345	431	347
427	351	425	353	354	422	356	420
417	361	415	363	364	412	366	410
370	406	372	404	403	375	401	377

$R = 4$

400	376	402	374	373	405	371	407
367	411	365	413	414	362	416	360
357	421	355	423	424	352	426	350
430	346	432	344	343	435	341	437
440	336	442	334	333	445	331	447
327	451	325	453	454	322	456	320
317	461	315	463	464	312	466	310
470	306	472	304	303	475	301	477

$R = 3$

500	276	502	274	273	505	271	507
267	511	265	513	514	262	516	260
257	521	255	523	524	252	526	250
530	246	532	244	243	535	241	537
540	236	542	234	233	545	231	547
227	551	225	553	554	222	556	220
217	561	215	563	564	212	566	210
570	206	572	204	203	575	201	577

$R = 2$

FIGURE 6–5 CONTINUED

177	601	175	603	604	172	606	170
610	166	612	164	163	615	161	617
620	156	622	154	153	625	151	627
147	631	145	633	634	142	636	140
137	641	135	643	644	132	646	130
650	126	652	124	123	655	121	657
660	116	662	114	113	665	111	667
107	671	105	673	674	102	676	100

R = 1

77	701	75	703	704	72	706	70
710	66	712	64	63	715	61	717
720	56	722	54	53	725	51	727
47	731	45	733	734	42	736	40
37	741	35	743	744	32	746	30
750	26	752	24	23	755	21	757
760	16	762	14	13	765	11	767
7	771	5	773	774	2	776	0

R = 0

FIGURE 6–5. PERFECT CUBE TO THE BASE 8

707	71	705	73	74	702	76	700
607	171	605	173	174	602	176	600
270	506	272	504	503	275	501	277
370	406	372	404	403	375	401	377
470	306	472	304	303	475	301	477
570	206	572	204	203	575	201	577
107	671	105	673	674	102	676	100
7	771	5	773	774	2	776	0

D = 0

FIGURE 6–6. FRONT ORTHOGONAL SECTION

777	10	20	747	737	50	60	707
677	110	120	647	637	150	160	607
200	567	557	230	240	527	517	270
300	467	457	330	340	427	417	370
400	367	357	430	440	327	317	470
500	267	257	530	540	227	217	570
177	610	620	147	137	650	660	107
77	710	720	47	37	750	760	7

C = 0

FIGURE 6–7. LEFT SIDE ORTHOGONAL SECTION

777	1	775	3	4	772	6	770
110	666	112	664	663	115	661	117
557	221	565	223	224	552	226	550
330	446	332	444	443	335	441	337
440	336	442	334	333	445	331	447
227	551	225	553	554	222	556	220
660	116	662	114	113	665	111	667
7	771	5	773	774	2	776	0

707	71	705	73	74	702	76	700
160	616	162	614	613	165	611	167
527	251	525	253	254	522	256	520
340	436	342	434	433	345	431	347
430	346	432	344	343	435	341	437
257	521	255	523	524	252	526	250
610	166	612	164	163	615	161	617
77	701	75	703	704	72	706	70

FIGURE 6–8. SPACE DIAGONALS

Examination of Figures 6–3 to 6–8 shows that they meet the requirements of a perfect cube:

(a) The numbers in every orthogonal add up to the magic constant.

(b) The numbers in the main diagonals of every orthogonal section add up to the magic constant.

(c) The numbers in all four space diagonals add up to the magic constant.

All that remains to convert this cube to a normal eighth-order perfect magic cube is to convert it to base 10 and add the number 1 to the number in each cell.

This method is much more general than it appears to be at first. Great liberties may be taken in the construction of the original natural-order cube. Let us consider the "units" digits first. It is not necessary to write the numbers in their natural order. Write the "units" digits 0 to 7, inclusive, in any orthogonal perpendicular to the left side. They may be written in any order you like so long as the numbers that are symmetrically located with respect to the center of the orthogonal add to $(N-1)=7$. For example, suppose you start with the third row in the top orthogonal section. Then the following order would be acceptable:

$$3 \quad 5 \quad 6 \quad 0 \quad 7 \quad 1 \quad 2 \quad 4.$$

Note that the sum of the first and last column, the sum of the second and next-to-last column, and so on, add to 7. Having selected the order for the "units" digits in the first orthogonal, you then must use the same order in all orthogonals parallel to it. There are 384 $(8 \times 6 \times 4 \times 2)$ different ways you may write the "units" digits in the first orthogonal.

Let us consider the "tens" digits next. They also may be written in any order you desire, the only difference being that now you must select one of the orthogonals perpendicular to the front of the cube. You must, of course, still meet the requirement that the numbers that are symmetrically located with respect to the center of the orthogonal add to $(N-1)=7$. For example, suppose you start with the left hand column in the top orthogonal section. Then the following order would be among the 384 possible:

$$6 \quad 3 \quad 2 \quad 0 \quad 7 \quad 5 \quad 4 \quad 1.$$

Having selected the order for the "tens" digits in the first orthogonal you then must use the same order in all parallel orthogonals.

Finally, we consider the "hundreds" digits. The procedure is now obvious. You may write the digits in any orthogonal perpendicular to the top, following any order you wish, provided that the numbers symmetrically located with respect to the center of the orthogonal add to $(N-1)=7$. Once again, you then must use the same order in all the remaining parallel orthogonals. Thus there are $384 \times 384 \times 384 = 56,623,104$ different ways in which you can write your original "natural-order" cube.

Although this method can produce an astonishing number of perfect magic cubes, as far as we know it is not possible to use it to construct a pandiagonal perfect magic cube.

We are now in a position to examine more critically the method employed by Barnard in describing the construction of the first perfect magic cube ever published. You may be surprised to note that it is a modification of the method we have just employed. By the use of elaborate, detailed, instructions, Barnard was able to omit the construction of the natural-order cube, but in so doing he lost all the flexibility that cube provides. Had he used such a cube and followed the transfer instructions given in Figure 6–9 for the first, fourth, fifth, and last orthogonal sections, and those in Figure 6–10 for the second, third, sixth, and seventh orthogonal sections, he would have constructed the identical perfect magic cube.

	X_1		X_2	X_2		X_1	
	X_3		X_4	X_4		X_3	
X_5		X_6			X_6		X_5
X_7		X_8			X_8		X_7
X_7		X_8			X_8		X_7
X_5		X_6			X_6		X_5
	X_3		X_4	X_4		X_3	
	X_1		X_2	X_2		X_1	

FIGURE 6–9. FIRST, FOURTH, FIFTH, AND LAST ORTHOGONAL SECTIONS

X_{11}		X_{12}			X_{12}		X_{11}
X_{13}		X_{14}			X_{14}		X_{13}
	X_{15}		X_{16}	X_{16}		X_{15}	
	X_{17}		X_{18}	X_{18}		X_{17}	
	X_{17}		X_{18}	X_{18}		X_{17}	
	X_{15}		X_{16}	X_{16}		X_{15}	
X_{13}		X_{14}			X_{14}		X_{13}
X_{11}		X_{12}			X_{12}		X_{11}

FIGURE 6–10. SECOND, THIRD, SIXTH, AND SEVENTH ORTHOGONAL SECTIONS

We now return to the cyclical method (and its intermediate cube that we developed in Chapters 2, 3, and 4 for lower order cubes.) We will take as Case 3 the following cube:

$$\begin{vmatrix} 1 & 2 & 0 \\ 2 & 0 & 1 \\ 0 & 1 & 2 \end{vmatrix}_N \quad \Delta = 9$$

Using the criteria given in Figure 3–3, it is easy to develop the controlling characteristics of the orthogonals (see Figure 6–11).

	x	X	x
Perpendicular to the side	1	4	-2
Perpendicular to the top	4	-2	1
Perpendicular to the front	-2	1	4

FIGURE 6–11. CONTROLLING CHARACTERISTICS OF THE ORTHOGONALS

We saw in Chapter 3 that the controlling characteristics for x in the main diagonals of the orthogonal sections were the sum and difference of each possible pair of the controlling characteristics for x (see Figure 6–11), that is, 1 ± 4, 1 ± 2, and 2 ± 4. This reduces to 5, -3, 3, -1, 6, and 2 or, what is the same thing, 1, 2, 3, 5, and 6 (as the controlling characteristic is independent of its sign). A glance at Figure 6–11 will show that the same values hold for X and x.

In Chapter 3 we also saw that the controlling characteristics for x in the space diagonals consisted of every possible sum and difference of these same controlling characteristics for x, that is, every possible value of $1 \pm 2 \pm 4$. This gives us -5, -1, 3, and 7, or, what is the same thing, 1, 3, 5, and 7. Here again these same values hold for X and x.

Since none of the controlling characteristics are 0 or a multiple of 8 (and since Δ is prime to 8), we predict we will be able to construct a pandiagonal perfect magic cube of the eighth order by using the generating characteristics of Case 3. We will, of course, find some duplications and omissions of letters whenever 2, 4, or 6 is the controlling characteristic. Since 8 is doubly even, however, we will have no difficulty in assigning values to the letters so as to make the orthogonals or diagonals in question magic.

Following the procedure outlined in Chapter 2 and using the Case 3 values for the generating characteristics, we will obtain the eight orthogonal sections parallel to the front of the cube (see Figure 6–12), the top orthogonal section (R = 7; see Figure 6–13), and the left side orthogonal section (C = 0; see Figure 6–14).

hCe	fGf	dCg	bGh	hCa	fGb	dCc	bGd
gEa	eAb	cEc	aAd	gEe	eAf	cEg	aAh
fGe	dCf	bGg	hCh	fGa	dCb	bGc	hCd
eAa	cEb	aAc	gEd	eAe	cEf	aAg	gEh
dCe	bGf	hCg	fGh	dCa	bGb	hCc	fGd
cEa	aAb	gEc	eAd	cEe	aAf	gEg	eAh
bGe	hCf	fGg	dCh	bGa	hCb	fGc	dCd
aAa	gEb	eAc	cEd	aAe	gEf	eAg	cEh

Front   D = 0

dDc	bHd	hDe	fHf	dDg	bHh	hDa	fHb
cFg	aBh	gFa	eBb	cFc	aBd	gFe	eBf
bHc	hDd	fHe	dDf	bHg	hDh	fHa	dDb
aBg	gFh	eBa	cFb	aBc	gFd	eBe	cFf
hDc	fHd	dDe	bHf	hDg	fHh	dDa	bHb
gFg	eBh	cFa	aBb	gFc	eBd	cFe	aBf
fHc	dDd	bHe	hDf	fHg	dDh	bHa	hDb
eBg	cFh	aBa	gFb	eBc	cFd	aBe	gFf

D = 1

FIGURE 6–12   CONTINUED

hEa	fAb	dEc	bAd	hEe	fAf	dEg	bAh
gGe	eCf	cGg	aCh	gGa	eCb	cGc	aCd
fAa	dEb	bAc	hEd	fAe	dEf	bAg	hEh
eCe	cGf	aCg	gGh	eCa	cGb	aCc	gGd
dEa	bAb	hEc	fAd	dEe	bAf	hEg	fAh
cGe	aCf	gGg	eCh	cGa	aCb	gGc	eCd
bAa	hEb	fAc	dEd	bAe	hEf	fAg	dEh
aCe	gGf	eCg	cGh	aCa	gGb	eCc	cGd

D = 2

dFg	bBh	hFa	fBb	dFc	bBd	hFe	fBf
cHc	aDd	gHe	eDf	cHg	aDh	gHa	eDb
bBg	hFh	fBa	dFb	bBc	hFd	fBe	dFf
aDc	gHd	eDe	cHf	aDg	gHh	eDa	cHb
hFg	fBh	dFa	bBb	hFc	fBd	dFe	bBf
gHc	eDd	cHe	aDf	gHg	eDh	cHa	aDb
fBg	dFh	bBa	hFb	fBc	dFd	bBe	hFf
eDc	cHd	aDe	gHf	eDg	cHh	aDa	gHb

D = 3

hGe	fCf	dGg	bCh	hGa	fCb	dGc	bCd
gAa	eEb	cAc	aEd	gAe	eEf	cAg	aEh
fCe	dGf	bCg	hGh	fCa	dGb	bCc	hGd
eEa	cAb	aEc	gAd	eEe	cAf	aEg	gAh
dGe	bCf	hGg	fCh	dGa	bCb	hGc	fCd
cAa	aEb	gAc	eEd	cAe	aEf	gAg	eEh
bCe	hGf	fCg	dGh	bCa	hGb	fCc	dGd
aEa	gAb	eEc	cAd	aEe	gAf	eEg	cAh

D = 4

FIGURE 6–12   CONTINUED

dHc	bDd	hHe	fDf	dHg	bDh	hHa	fDb
cBg	aFh	gBa	eFb	cBc	aFd	gBe	eFf
bDc	hHd	fDe	dHf	bDg	hHh	fDa	dHb
aFg	gBh	eFa	cBb	aFc	gBd	eFe	cBf
hHc	fDd	dHe	bDf	hHg	fDh	dHa	bDb
gBg	eFh	cBa	aFb	gBc	eFd	cBe	aFf
fDc	dHd	bDe	hHf	fDg	dHh	bDa	hHb
eFg	cBh	aFa	gBb	eFc	cBd	aFe	gBf

D = 5

hAa	fEb	dAc	bEd	hAe	fEf	dAg	bEh
gCe	eGf	cCg	aGh	gCa	eGb	cCc	aGd
fEa	dAb	bEc	hAd	fEe	dAf	bEg	hAh
eGe	cCf	aGg	gCh	eGa	cCb	aGc	gCd
dAa	bEb	hAc	fEd	dAe	bEf	hAg	fEh
cCe	aGf	gCg	eGh	cCa	aGb	gCc	eGd
bEa	hAb	fEc	dAd	bEe	hAf	fEg	dAh
aGe	gCf	eGg	cCh	aGa	gCb	eGc	cCd

D = 6

dBg	bFh	hBa	fFb	dBc	bFd	hBe	fFf
cDc	aHd	gDe	eHf	cDg	aHh	gDa	eHb
bFg	hBh	fFa	dBb	bFc	hBd	fFe	dBf
aHc	gDd	eHe	cDf	aHg	gDh	eHa	cDb
hBg	fFh	dBa	bFb	hBc	fFd	dBe	bFf
gDc	eHd	cDe	aHf	gDg	eHh	cDa	aHb
fFg	dBh	bFa	hBb	fFc	dBd	bFe	hBf
eHc	cDd	aHe	gDf	eHg	cDh	aHa	gDb

D = 7

FIGURE 6–12. EIGHT ORTHOGONAL SECTIONS PARALLEL TO THE FRONT OF AN 8 × 8 × 8 PANDIAGONAL PERFECT MAGIC CUBE

dBg	bFh	hBa	fFb	dBc	bFd	hBe	fFf
hAa	fEb	dAc	bEd	hAe	fEf	dAg	bEh
dHc	bDd	hHe	fDf	dHg	bDh	hHa	fDb
hGe	fCf	dGg	bCh	hGa	fCb	dGc	bCd
dFg	bBh	hFa	fBb	dFc	bBd	hFe	fBf
hEa	fAb	dEc	bAd	hEe	fAf	dEg	bAh
dDc	bHd	hDe	fHf	dDg	bHh	hDa	fHb
hCe	fGf	dCg	bGh	hCa	fGb	dCc	bGd

R = 7

FIGURE 6–13. TOP ORTHOGONAL SECTION

dBg	hAa	dHc	hGe	dFg	hEa	dDc	hCe
cDc	gCe	cBg	gAa	cHc	gGe	cFg	gEa
bFg	fEa	bDc	fCe	bBg	fAa	bHc	fGe
aHc	eGe	aFg	eEa	aDc	eCe	aBg	eAa
hBg	dAa	hHc	dGe	hFg	dEa	hDc	dCe
gDc	cCe	gBg	cAa	gHc	cGe	gFg	cEa
fFg	bEa	fDc	bCe	fBg	bAa	fHc	bGe
eHc	aGe	eFg	aEa	eDc	aCe	eBg	aAa

C = 0

FIGURE 6–14. LEFT SIDE ORTHOGONAL SECTION

Figures 6–12 through 6–14 show that whenever the controlling characteristic is 1, each letter appears once and only once; when it is 2 (or 6), four letters appear twice each; when it is 4, two letters appear four times each. Note also that whenever the capital letters appear in pairs they are A and E, B and F, C and G, and D and H. Further, whenever the capital letters appear in groups of four they are either A, C, E, and G or B, D, F, and H. It follows that if we let $A + E = B + F = C + G = D + H = 7$, all of the orthogonals and diagonals will be magic. The same conditions hold for the lowercase and italic letters.

If we let $A = a = a = 0$, $B = b = b = 1$, $C = c = c = 2$, $D = d = d = 3$, $E = e = e = 7$, $F = f = f = 6$, $G = g = g = 5$, and $H = h = h = 4$, and substitute these values in Figures 6–12, 6–13, and 6–14, we will generate Figure 6–15 (the front orthogonal section, $D = 0$), Figure 6–16 (the top orthogonal section, $R = 7$), and Figure 6–17 (the left side orthogonal section, $C = 0$). The construction of the remaining orthogonal sections follows in a perfectly straightforward manner and is left to the interested reader. To check two of the space diagonals we have only to look at Figures 6–18 and 6–19, which show a diagonal section perpendicular to the left side.

427	656	325	154	720	651	322	153
570	701	272	3	577	706	275	4
657	326	155	424	650	321	152	423
700	271	2	573	707	276	5	574
327	156	425	654	320	151	422	653
270	1	572	703	277	6	575	704
157	426	655	324	150	421	652	323
0	571	702	273	7	576	705	274

$$D = 0$$

FIGURE 6–15. FRONT ORTHOGONAL SECTION

315	164	410	661	312	163	417	666
400	671	302	173	407	676	305	174
342	133	447	636	345	134	440	631
457	626	355	124	450	621	352	123
365	114	460	611	362	113	467	616
470	601	372	103	477	606	375	104
332	143	437	646	335	144	430	641
427	656	325	154	420	651	322	153

Top $R = 7$

FIGURE 6–16. TOP ORTHOGONAL SECTION

315	400	342	457	365	470	332	427
232	527	215	500	242	557	265	570
165	670	132	627	115	600	142	657
42	757	65	770	32	727	15	700
415	300	442	357	465	370	432	327
532	227	515	200	542	257	565	270
665	170	632	127	615	100	642	157
742	57	765	70	732	27	715	0

$C = 0$

FIGURE 6–17. LEFT SIDE ORTHOGONAL SECTION

hCe	fGf	dCg	bGh	hCa	fGb	dCc	bGd
cFg	aBh	gFa	eBb	cFc	aBd	gFe	eBf
fAa	dEb	bAc	hEd	fAe	dEf	bAg	hEh
aDc	gHd	eDe	cHf	aDg	gHh	eDa	cHb
dGe	bCf	hGg	fCh	dGa	bCb	hGc	fCd
gBg	eFh	cBa	aFb	gBc	eFd	cBe	aFf
bEa	hAb	fEc	dAd	bEe	hAf	fEg	dAh
eHc	cDd	aHe	gDf	eHg	cDh	aHa	gDb

FIGURE 6–18. SPACE DIAGONAL SECTION PERPENDICULAR TO LEFT SIDE

Figures 6–12 through 6–19 show that the orthogonal sections and the diagonal section are indeed pandiagonal magic squares; thus the cube will be a pandiagonal perfect magic cube. Figure 6–12 shows that this cube has another rather basic magic property, namely, that the total of the eight numbers in *any* $2 \times 2 \times 2$ subcube equals 4 times $(N^3 - 1)$ or, in this case, 4×777, equal to the magic constant in the case of the eighth-order cube.

This property of the second-order subcubes could have been predicted; it holds for any cube constructed from generating characteristics where at least one of the controlling characteristics for x, X, and x equals $N/2$. Case 2 meets this requirement and Figure 3–7 shows that the cube has the sum of the eight

427	656	325	154	420	651	322	153
265	14	560	711	262	13	567	716
600	371	102	473	607	376	105	474
32	543	737	246	35	544	730	241
357	126	455	624	350	121	452	623
515	764	210	61	512	763	217	66
170	401	672	303	177	406	675	304
742	233	47	536	745	234	40	531

FIGURE 6–19. SPACE DIAGONAL SECTION PERPENDICULAR TO LEFT SIDE

numbers in any $2 \times 2 \times 2$ subcube equal to $4 \times 333 = 4$ times $(N^3 - 1)$.

This remarkable pandiagonal perfect magic cube has the additional property that the numbers in the eight corners of any $3 \times 3 \times 3$, $4 \times 4 \times 4$, $5 \times 5 \times 5$, $6 \times 6 \times 6$, or $7 \times 7 \times 7$ subcube lying within it also have a sum equal to the magic constant, 2,052. Incidentally, the sum of the numbers in the eight corners of the main $8 \times 8 \times 8$ cube is also 2,052.

Chapter 7

Seventh-Order Magic Cubes

Now that we are constructing a seventh-order magic cube, we should be in a position to reap some of the benefits of our previous work. We could use the generating characteristics of Cases 1 and 2, but we are looking for more than a simple pandiagonal magic cube. How about Case 3? You will recall its elements:

$$\begin{vmatrix} 1 & 2 & 0 \\ 2 & 0 & 1 \\ 0 & 1 & 2 \end{vmatrix}_N \quad \Delta = 9$$

Since all of the controlling characteristics except the 7 in the space diagonals are prime to 7 (see Figure 7–1), we know in advance that a cube generated using these characteristics will have every orthogonal section be a pandiagonal magic square and every orthogonal will be correct, as will all the space diagonals, except those whose controlling characteristic is 7. We can make the space diagonal going through the center of the cube correct by proper assignment of values to the letters, but

For orthogonals	1 2 4
For diagonals in orthogonal sections	1 2 3 5 6
For space diagonals	1 3 5 7

FIGURE 7–1. CONTROLLING CHARACTERISTICS

since it is not possible to make all of the broken diagonals correct, the cube we generate will be perfect but not pandiagonally perfect.

Can we do any better with another set of generating characteristics? No, we cannot. Following the same analytical procedure we used in Chapter 4, we see that we must use as our orthogonal controlling characteristics a set of three different numbers selected from 1 to 6, inclusive, and that the set must have the following properties: no combination of any two of the three numbers has a sum or difference equal to 0 or to a multiple of 7, and no possible combination of any three is equal to 0 or to a multiple of 7. If the numbers fail to meet the first requirement, at least one set of diagonals in the orthogonal sections will be incorrect (the set will consist of one of the letters repeated seven times). If the numbers do not meet the second requirement, the space diagonals will fail for a similar reason.

Let us look at a few of the possible combinations:

(1)   1, 2, 3 fails because $1 + 2 - 3 = 0$.
(2)   1, 2, 4 fails because $1 + 2 + 4 = 7$.
(3)   1, 2, 5 fails because $2 + 5 = 7$.
(4)   1, 2, 6 fails because $1 + 6 = 7$.

An examination of all the possible combinations shows that none work. Thus using this method makes it simple to find a set of generating characteristics for a pandiagonal or a perfect magic cube, but it is not possible to generate a seventh-order pandiagonal perfect magic cube. This being the case, let us stick with the characteristics in Case 3 and use them to construct our seventh-order perfect magic cube.

Also, we know that the cube will be correct if we start with the number 0 in the proper cell so that the number 333 (where 333 to the base 7 equals $3(7^2) + 3(7) + 3 = 171$—the mean of the numbers 0 to 342, inclusive) falls in the center cell. Since we are not looking for a complicated substitution of values for the letters, let us generate the cube directly without the aid of the intermediate letter cube. All that is necessary to locate the proper starting point is to work backward from the center.

To have the number 333 in the center cell we will need the number 222 in the cell three columns to the left, three rows down, and three cells out (in the negative direction for D). The reason for this is that to find the cell occupied by a number one digit larger in the "hundreds," "tens," and "units" places, all you need to do is to move $(C+c+c)$ cells to the right (three cells in our case), $(R+r+r)$ rows up (three rows in our case), and $(D+d+d)$ cells in (three cells in our case). Repeating this process to locate first the number 111 and then the number 0, we find that our proper starting point is the cell in the second column $(C=1)$, second row $(R=1)$, and second plane from the front $(D=1)$.

We therefore start with 0 in cell [1,1,1] and, following our normal procedure, generate the orthogonal sections parallel to the front (see Figure 7–2), the orthogonal sections parallel to the top (see Figure 7–3), the orthogonal sections parallel to the side (Figure 7–4), and the diagonal sections perpendicular to the left side of the cube (Figure 7–5). These sections have the predicted properties; thus we have constructed a seventh-order perfect magic cube.

530	454	301	225	142	66	613
145	62	616	533	450	304	221
453	300	224	141	65	612	536
61	615	532	456	303	220	144
306	223	140	64	611	535	452
614	531	455	302	226	143	60
222	146	63	610	534	451	305

Front D = 0

6	623	540	464	311	235	152
314	231	155	2	626	543	460
622	546	463	310	234	151	5
230	154	1	625	542	466	313
545	462	316	233	150	4	621
153	0	624	541	465	312	236
461	315	232	156	3	620	544

D = 1

245	162	16	633	550	404	321
553	400	324	241	165	12	636
161	15	632	556	403	320	244
406	323	240	164	11	635	552
14	631	555	402	326	243	160
322	246	163	10	634	551	405
630	554	401	325	242	166	13

D = 2

414	331	255	102	26	643	560
22	646	563	410	334	251	105
330	254	101	25	642	566	413
645	562	416	333	250	104	21
253	100	24	641	565	412	336
561	415	332	256	103	20	644
106	23	640	564	411	335	252

D = 3

653	500	424	341	265	112	36
261	115	32	656	503	420	344
506	423	340	264	111	35	652
114	31	655	502	426	343	260
422	346	263	110	34	651	505
30	654	501	425	342	266	113
345	262	116	33	650	504	421

D = 4

122	46	663	510	434	351	205
430	354	201	125	42	666	513
45	662	516	433	350	204	121
353	200	124	41	665	512	436
661	515	432	356	203	120	44
206	123	40	664	511	435	352
514	431	355	202	126	43	660

D = 5

361	215	132	56	603	520	444
606	523	440	364	211	135	52
214	131	55	602	526	443	360
522	446	363	210	134	51	605
130	54	601	525	442	366	213
445	362	216	133	50	604	521
53	600	524	441	365	212	136

Back D = 6

FIGURE 7–2. ORTHOGONAL SECTIONS PARALLEL TO THE FRONT

361	215	132	56	603	520	444
122	46	663	510	434	351	205
653	500	424	341	265	112	36
414	331	255	102	26	643	560
245	162	16	633	550	404	321
6	623	540	464	311	235	152
530	454	301	225	142	66	613

Top R = 6

606	523	440	364	211	135	52
430	354	201	125	42	666	513
261	115	32	656	503	420	344
22	646	563	410	334	251	105
553	400	324	241	165	12	636
314	231	155	2	626	543	460
145	62	616	533	450	304	221

R = 5

214	131	55	602	526	443	360
45	662	516	433	350	204	121
506	423	340	264	111	35	652
330	254	101	25	642	566	413
161	15	632	556	403	320	244
622	546	463	310	234	151	5
453	300	224	141	65	612	536

R = 4

522	446	363	210	134	51	605
353	200	124	41	665	512	436
114	31	655	502	426	343	260
645	562	416	333	250	104	21
406	323	240	164	11	635	552
230	154	1	625	542	466	313
61	615	532	456	303	220	144

R = 3

130	54	601	525	442	366	213
661	515	432	356	203	120	44
422	346	263	110	34	651	505
253	100	24	641	565	412	336
14	631	555	402	326	243	160
545	462	316	233	150	4	621
306	223	140	64	611	535	452

R = 2

445	362	216	133	50	604	521
206	123	40	664	511	435	352
30	654	501	425	342	266	113
561	415	332	256	103	20	644
322	246	163	10	634	551	405
153	0	624	541	465	312	236
614	531	455	302	226	143	60

R = 1

53	600	524	441	365	212	136
514	431	355	202	126	43	660
345	262	116	33	650	504	421
106	23	640	564	411	335	252
630	554	401	325	242	166	13
461	315	232	156	3	620	544
222	146	63	610	534	451	305

Bottom R = 0

FIGURE 7–3. ORTHOGONAL SECTIONS PARALLEL TO THE TOP

361	122	653	414	245	6	530
606	430	261	22	553	314	145
214	45	506	330	161	622	453
522	353	114	645	406	230	61
130	661	422	253	14	545	306
445	206	30	561	322	153	614
53	514	345	106	630	461	222

Left side C = 0

215	46	500	331	162	623	454
523	354	115	646	400	231	62
131	662	423	254	15	546	300
446	200	31	562	323	154	615
54	515	346	100	631	462	223
362	123	654	415	246	0	531
600	431	262	23	554	315	146

C = 1

132	663	424	255	16	540	301
440	201	32	563	324	155	616
55	516	340	101	632	463	224
363	124	655	416	240	1	532
601	432	263	24	555	316	140
216	40	501	332	163	624	455
524	355	116	640	401	232	63

C = 2

56	510	341	102	633	464	225
364	125	656	410	241	2	533
602	433	264	25	556	310	141
210	41	502	333	164	625	456
525	356	110	641	402	233	64
133	664	425	256	10	541	302
441	202	33	564	325	156	610

C = 3

603	434	265	26	550	311	142
211	42	503	334	165	626	450
526	350	111	642	403	234	65
134	665	426	250	11	542	303
449	203	34	565	326	150	611
50	511	342	103	634	465	226
365	126	650	411	242	3	534

C = 4

520	351	112	643	404	235	66
135	666	420	251	12	543	304
443	204	35	566	320	151	612
51	512	343	104	635	466	220
366	120	651	412	243	4	535
604	435	266	20	551	312	143
212	43	504	335	166	620	451

C = 5

444	205	36	560	321	152	613
52	513	344	105	636	460	221
360	121	652	413	244	5	536
605	436	260	21	552	313	144
213	44	505	336	160	621	452
521	352	113	644	405	236	60
136	660	421	252	13	544	305

Right side C = 6

FIGURE 7–4. ORTHOGONAL SECTIONS PARALLEL TO THE SIDE

530	454	301	225	142	66	613
314	231	155	2	626	543	460
161	15	632	556	403	320	244
645	562	416	333	250	104	21
422	346	263	110	34	651	505
206	123	40	664	511	435	352
53	600	524	441	365	212	136

222	146	63	610	534	451	305
153	0	624	541	465	312	236
14	631	555	402	326	243	160
645	562	416	333	250	104	21
506	423	340	264	111	35	652
430	354	201	125	42	666	513
361	215	132	56	603	520	444

FIGURE 7–5. DIAGONAL SECTIONS PERPENDICULAR TO LEFT SIDE

Chapter 8

Ninth-Order Magic Cubes

Since we are interested here in pandiagonal perfect magic cubes, we have no use for the generating characteristics in Cases 1 and 2. Also, since Δ equals 9, we cannot use those of Case 3. Thus we shall consider a slight variation of Case 3, which we shall call Case 4:

$$\begin{vmatrix} 1 & -2 & 0 \\ -2 & 0 & 1 \\ 0 & 1 & -2 \end{vmatrix}_N \qquad \Delta = -7$$

The controlling characteristics (see Figure 8–1) for the diagonals in the orthogonal section are, as for Case 3, 1, 2, 3, 5, and 6 and, similarly, the controlling characteristics for the space diagonals are 1, 3, 5, and 7. Since 9 is prime to Δ and since none of the controlling characteristics are 0 or a multiple of 9, we can indeed construct our cube. All orthogonals and diagonals, except those where the controlling characteristic is 3 or 6, will automatically be magic since each letter appears once and only once. In the excepted cases each orthogonal and diagonal will consist of three different letters, each appearing three times $(9/3 = 3)$.

	x	X	x
Perpendicular to the side	1	4	2
Perpendicular to the top	4	2	1
Perpendicular to the front	2	1	4

FIGURE 8–1. CONTROLLING CHARACTERISTICS OF THE ORTHOGONALS FOR CASE 4

dHg	eAc	fCh	gEd	hGi	iIe	aBa	bDf	cFb
hGe	iIa	aBf	bDb	cFg	dHc	eAh	fCd	gEi
cFc	dHh	eAd	fCi	gEe	hGa	iIf	aBb	bDg
gEa	hGf	iIb	aBg	bDc	cFh	dHd	eAi	fCe
bDh	cFd	dHi	eAe	fCa	gEf	hGb	iIg	aBc
fCf	gEb	hGg	iIc	aBh	bDd	cFi	dHe	eAa
aBd	bDi	cFe	dHa	eAf	fCb	gEg	hGc	iIh
eAb	fCg	gEc	hGh	iId	aBi	bDe	cFa	dHf
iIi	aBe	bDa	cFf	dHb	eAg	fCc	gEh	hGd

Front D = 0

fDh	gFd	hHi	iAe	aCa	bEf	cGb	dIg	eBc
aCf	bEb	cGg	dIc	eBh	fDd	gFi	hHe	iAa
eBd	fDi	gFe	hHa	iAf	aCb	bEg	cGc	dIh
iAb	aCg	bEc	cGh	dId	eBi	fDe	gFa	hHf
dIi	eBe	fDa	gFf	hHb	iAg	aCc	bEh	cGd
hHg	iAc	aCh	bEd	cGi	dIe	eBa	fDf	gFb
cGe	dIa	eBf	fDb	gFg	hHc	iAh	aCd	bEi
gFc	hHh	iAd	aCi	bEe	cGa	dIf	eBb	fDg
bEa	cGf	dIb	eBg	fDc	gFh	hHd	iAi	aCe

D = 1

hIi	iBe	aDa	bFf	cHb	dAg	eCc	fEh	gGd
cHg	dAc	eCh	fEd	gGi	hIe	iBa	aDf	bFb
gGe	hIa	iBf	aDb	bFg	cHc	dAh	eCd	fEi
bFc	cHh	dAd	eCi	fEe	gGa	hIf	iBb	aDg
fEa	gGf	hIb	iBg	aDc	bFh	cHd	dAi	eCe
aDh	bFd	cHi	dAe	eCa	fEf	gGb	hIg	iBc
eCf	fEb	gGg	hIc	iBh	aDd	bFi	cHe	dAa
iBd	aDi	bFe	cHa	dAf	eCb	fEg	gGc	hIh
dAb	eCg	fEc	gGh	hId	iBi	aDe	bFa	cHf

D = 2

FIGURE 8–2 CONTINUED

aEa	bGf	cIb	dBg	eDc	fFh	gHd	hAi	iCe
eDh	fFd	gHi	hAe	iCa	aEf	bGb	cIg	dBc
iCf	aEb	bGg	cIc	dBh	eDd	fFi	gHe	hAa
dBd	eDi	fFe	gHa	hAf	iCb	aEg	bGc	cIh
hAb	iCg	aEc	bGh	cId	dBi	eDe	fFa	gHf
cIi	dBe	eDa	fFf	gHb	hAg	iCc	aEh	bGd
gHg	hAc	iCh	aEd	bGi	cIe	dBa	eDf	fFb
bGe	cIa	dBf	eDb	fFg	gHc	hAh	iCd	aEi
fFc	gHh	hAd	iCi	aEe	bGa	cIf	dBb	eDg

D = 3

cAb	dCg	eEc	fGh	gId	hBi	iDe	aFa	bHf
gIi	hBe	iDa	aFf	bHb	cAg	dCc	eEh	fGd
bHg	cAc	dCh	eEd	fGi	gIe	hBa	iDf	aFb
fGe	gIa	hBf	iDb	aFg	bHc	cAh	dCd	eEi
aFc	bHh	cAd	dCi	eEe	fGa	gIf	hBb	iDg
eEa	fGf	gIb	hBg	iDc	aFh	bHd	cAi	dCe
iDh	aFd	bHi	cAe	dCa	eEf	fGb	gIg	hBc
dCf	eEb	fGg	gIc	hBh	iDd	aFi	bHe	cAa
hBd	iDi	aFe	bHa	cAf	dCb	eEg	fGc	gIh

D = 4

eFc	fHh	gAd	hCi	iEe	aGa	bIf	cBb	dDg
iEa	aGf	bIb	cBg	dDc	eFh	fHd	gAi	hCe
dDh	eFd	fHi	gAe	hCa	iEf	aGb	bIg	cBc
hCf	iEb	aGg	bIc	cBh	dDd	eFi	fHe	gAa
cBd	dDi	eFe	fHa	gAf	hCb	iEg	aGc	bIh
gAb	hCg	iEc	aGh	bId	cBi	dDe	eFa	fHf
bIi	cBe	dDa	eFf	fHb	gAg	hCc	iEh	aGd
fHg	gAc	hCh	iEd	aGi	bIe	cBa	dDf	eFb
aGe	bIa	cBf	dDb	eFg	fHc	gAh	hCd	iEi

D = 5

FIGURE 8–2 CONTINUED

gBd	hDi	iFe	aHa	bAf	cCb	dEg	eGc	fIh
bAb	cCg	dEc	eGh	fId	gBi	hDe	iFa	aHf
fIi	gBe	hDa	iFf	aHb	bAg	cCc	dEh	eGd
aHg	bAc	cCh	dEd	eGi	fIe	gBa	hDf	iFb
eGe	fIa	gBf	hDb	iFg	aHc	bAh	cCd	dEi
iFc	aHh	bAd	cCi	dEe	eGa	fIf	gBb	hDg
dEa	eGf	fIb	gBg	hDc	iFh	aHd	bAi	cCe
hDh	iFd	aHi	bAe	cCa	dEf	eGb	fIg	gBc
cCf	dEb	eGg	fIc	gBh	hDd	iFi	aHe	bAa

$$D = 6$$

iGe	aIa	bBf	cDb	dFg	eHc	fAh	gCd	hEi
dFc	eHh	fAd	gCi	hEe	iGa	aIf	bBb	cDg
hEa	iGf	aIb	bBg	cDc	dFh	eHd	fAi	gCe
cDh	dGd	eHi	fAe	gCa	hEf	iGb	aIg	bBc
gCf	hEb	iGg	aIc	bBh	cDd	dFi	eHe	fAa
bBd	cDi	dFe	eHa	fAf	gCb	hEg	iGc	aIh
fAb	gCg	hEc	iGh	aId	bBi	cDe	dFa	eHf
aIi	bBe	cDa	dFf	eHb	fAg	gCc	hEh	iGd
eHg	fAc	gCh	hEd	iGi	aIe	bBa	cDf	dFb

$$D = 7$$

bCf	cEb	dGg	eIc	fBh	gDd	hFi	iHe	aAa
fBd	gDi	hFe	iHa	aAf	bCb	cEg	dGc	eIh
aAb	bCg	cEc	dGh	eId	fBi	gDe	hFa	iHf
eIi	fBe	gDa	hFf	iHb	aAg	bCc	cEh	dGd
iHg	aAc	bCh	cEd	dGi	eIe	fBa	gDf	hFb
dGe	eIa	fBf	gDb	hFg	iHc	aAh	bCd	cEi
hFc	iHh	aAd	bCi	cEe	dGa	eIf	fBb	gDg
cEa	dGf	eIb	fBg	gDc	hFh	iHd	aAi	bCe
gDh	hFd	iHi	aAe	bCa	cEf	dGb	eIg	fBc

Back $D = 8$

FIGURE 8–2. ORTHOGONAL SECTIONS PARALLEL TO THE FRONT

bCf	cEb	dGg	eIc	fBh	gDd	hFi	iHe	aAa
iGe	aIa	bBf	cDb	dFg	eHc	fAh	gCd	hEi
gBd	hDi	iFe	aHa	bAf	cCb	dEg	eGc	fIh
eFc	fHh	gAd	hCi	iEe	aGa	bIf	cBb	dDg
cAb	dCg	eEc	fGh	gId	hBi	iDe	aFa	bHf
aEa	bGf	cIb	dBg	eDc	fFh	gHd	hAi	iCe
hIi	iBe	aDa	bFf	cHb	dAg	eCc	fEh	gGd
fDh	gFd	hHi	iAe	aCa	bEf	cGb	dIg	eBc
dHg	eAc	fCh	gEd	hGi	iIe	aBa	bDf	cFb

R = 8

FIGURE 8–3 TOP ORTHOGONAL SECTION

bCf	iGe	gBd	eFc	cAb	aEa	hIi	fDh	dHg
fBd	dFc	bAb	iEa	gIi	eDh	cHg	aCf	hGe
aAb	hEa	fIi	dDh	bHg	iCf	gGe	eBd	cFc
eIi	cDh	aHg	hCf	fGe	dBd	bFc	iAb	gEa
iHg	gCf	eGe	cBd	aFc	hAb	fEa	dIi	bDh
dGe	bBd	iFc	gAb	eEa	cIi	aDh	hHg	fCf
hFc	fAb	dEa	bIi	iDh	gHg	eCf	cGe	aBd
cEa	aIi	hDh	fHg	dCf	bGe	iBd	gFc	eAb
gDh	eHg	cCf	aGe	hBd	fFc	dAb	bEa	iIi

C = 0

FIGURE 8–4. LEFT SIDE ORTHOGONAL SECTION

gDh	hFd	iHi	aAe	bCa	cEf	dGb	eIg	fBc
ali	bBe	cDa	dFf	eHb	fAg	gCc	hEh	iGd
dEa	eGf	fIb	gBg	hDc	iFh	aHd	bAi	cCe
gAb	hCg	iEc	aGh	bId	cBi	dDe	eFa	fHf
aFc	bHh	cAd	dCi	eEe	fGa	gIf	hBb	iDg
dBd	eDi	fFe	gHa	hAf	iCb	aEg	bGc	cIh
gGe	hIa	iBf	aDb	bFg	cHc	dAh	eCd	fEi
aCf	bEb	cGg	dIc	eBh	fDd	gFi	hHe	iAa
dHg	eAc	fCh	gEd	hGi	iIe	aBa	bDf	cFb

iIi	aBe	bDa	cFf	dHb	eAg	fCc	gEh	hGd
gFc	hHh	iAd	aCi	bEe	cGa	dIf	eBb	fDg
eCf	fEb	gGg	hIc	iBh	aDd	bFi	cHe	dAa
cIi	dBe	eDa	fFf	gHb	hAg	iCc	aEh	bGd
aFc	bHh	cAd	dCi	eEe	fGa	gIf	hBb	iDg
hCf	iEb	aGg	bIc	cBh	dDd	eFi	fHe	gAa
fIi	gBe	hDa	iFf	aHb	bAg	cCc	dEh	eGd
dFc	eHh	fAd	gCi	hEe	iGa	aIf	bBb	cDg
bCf	cEb	dGg	eIc	fBh	gDd	hFi	iHe	aAa

FIGURE 8–5. DIAGONAL SECTIONS PERPENDICULAR TO LEFT SIDE
SHOWING SPACE DIAGONALS

Following our standard procedure, we generate the orthogonal sections parallel to the front (see Figure 8–2), the top orthogonal section (Figure 8–3), the left side orthogonal section (Figure 8–4), and the diagonal sections perpendicular to the left side (Figure 8–5). These sections have the predicted properties and whenever the orthogonal consists of only three letters, each repeated three times, these letters appear in the same groups, namely, A, D, G or B, E, H or C, F, I. It is easy to assign values to the various letters so that each of these three groups will have the same totals:

$$2 + 4 + 6 = 1 + 3 + 8 = 0 + 5 + 7 = 12, \quad \text{and}$$

$$1 + 5 + 6 = 0 + 4 + 8 = 2 + 3 + 7 = 12.$$

Either will work, but notice that if we make

$$A + I = B + H = C + G = D + F = 8 \quad \text{and} \quad E = 4,$$

$$a + i = b + h = c + g = d + f = 8 \quad \text{and} \quad e = 4, \quad \text{and}$$

$$a + i = b + h = c + g = d + f = 8 \quad \text{and} \quad e = 4,$$

our cube will not only be a pandiagonal perfect magic cube but will be symmetrical whenever the number $444 = 4(9^2) + 4(9) + 4 = 364 = (9^3 - 1)/2$ is in the center cell.

There are, of course, many different ways to assign the numbers and meet the necessary conditions. All that is necessary to generate the desired cube is to assign values to the letters, convert to the base 10, and then add 1 to the number in each cell.

Although it is not necessary, let us use the same values for each set of letters since it makes the actual construction of the cube easier.

$$a = A = a = 1, \quad b = B = b = 0, \qquad c = C = c = 2,$$
$$d = D = e = 5, \quad e = E = e = 4, \qquad f = F = f = 3,$$
$$g = G = g = 6, \quad h = H = h = 8, \quad \text{and} \quad i = I = i = 7,$$

Note that these values meet the requirements stated above. Substituting these values into Figures 8–2 through 8–5 gives us the orthogonal sections parallel to the front (see Figure 8–6), the top orthogonal section (Figure 8–7), the left side orthogonal section (Figure 8–8), and the diagonal sections perpendicular to the left side (Figure 8–9). Since these figures are to the base 9, it is easy to check that the cube has the properties predicted and is a symmetrical pandiagonal perfect magic cube. The digits in each series of "hundreds," "tens," and "units" will either appear once and only once (and thus add to 36) or will be three digits (each repeated three times) that add to 36.

586	412	328	645	867	774	101	53	230
864	771	103	50	236	582	418	325	647
232	588	415	327	644	861	773	100	56
641	863	770	106	52	238	585	417	324
58	235	587	414	321	643	860	776	102
323	640	866	772	108	55	237	584	411
105	57	234	581	413	320	646	862	778
410	326	642	868	775	107	54	231	583
777	104	51	233	580	416	322	648	865

Front D = 0

358	635	887	714	121	43	260	576	402
123	40	266	572	408	355	637	884	711
405	357	634	881	713	120	46	262	578
710	126	42	268	575	407	354	631	883
577	404	351	633	880	716	122	48	265
886	712	128	45	267	574	401	353	630
264	571	403	350	636	882	718	125	47
632	888	715	127	44	261	573	400	356
41	263	570	406	352	638	885	717	124

D = 1

877	704	151	33	280	516	422	348	665
286	512	428	345	667	874	701	153	30
664	871	703	150	36	282	518	425	347
32	288	515	427	344	661	873	700	156
341	663	870	706	152	38	285	517	424
158	35	287	514	421	343	660	876	702
423	340	666	872	708	155	37	284	511
705	157	34	281	513	420	346	662	878
510	426	342	668	875	707	154	31	283

D = 2

FIGURE 8–6 CONTINUED

141	63	270	506	452	338	685	817	724
458	335	687	814	721	143	60	276	502
723	140	66	272	508	455	337	684	811
505	457	334	681	813	720	146	62	278
810	726	142	68	275	507	454	331	683
277	504	451	333	680	816	722	148	65
686	812	728	145	67	274	501	453	330
64	271	503	450	336	682	818	725	147
332	688	815	727	144	61	273	500	456

$$D = 3$$

210	526	442	368	675	807	754	131	83
677	804	751	133	80	216	522	448	365
86	212	528	445	367	674	801	753	130
364	671	803	750	136	82	218	525	447
132	88	215	527	444	361	673	800	756
441	363	670	806	752	138	85	217	524
758	135	87	214	521	443	360	676	802
523	440	366	672	808	755	137	84	211
805	757	134	81	213	520	446	362	678

$$D = 4$$

432	388	615	827	744	161	73	200	556
741	163	70	206	552	438	385	617	824
558	435	387	614	821	743	160	76	202
823	740	166	72	208	555	437	384	611
205	557	434	381	613	820	746	162	78
610	826	742	168	75	207	554	431	383
77	204	551	433	380	616	822	748	165
386	612	828	745	167	74	201	553	430
164	71	203	550	436	382	618	825	747

$$D = 5$$

FIGURE 8–6 CONTINUED

605	857	734	181	13	220	546	462	378
10	226	542	468	375	607	854	731	183
377	604	851	733	180	16	222	548	465
186	12	228	545	467	374	601	853	730
464	371	603	850	736	182	18	225	547
732	188	15	227	544	461	373	600	856
541	463	370	606	852	738	185	17	224
858	735	187	14	221	543	460	376	602
223	540	466	372	608	855	737	184	11

$D = 6$

764	171	3	250	536	482	318	625	847
532	488	315	627	844	761	173	0	256
841	763	170	6	252	538	485	317	624
258	535	487	314	621	843	760	176	2
623	840	766	172	8	255	537	484	311
5	257	534	481	313	620	846	762	178
310	626	842	768	175	7	254	531	483
177	4	251	533	480	316	622	848	765
486	312	628	845	767	174	1	253	530

$D = 7$

23	240	566	472	308	655	837	784	111
305	657	834	781	113	20	246	562	478
110	26	242	568	475	307	654	831	783
477	304	651	833	780	116	22	248	565
786	112	28	245	567	474	301	653	830
564	471	303	650	836	782	118	25	247
832	788	115	27	244	561	473	300	656
241	563	470	306	652	838	785	117	24
658	835	787	114	21	243	560	476	302

Back $D = 8$

FIGURE 8–6. ORTHOGONAL SECTIONS PARALLEL TO THE FRONT OF A
$9 \times 9 \times 9$ SYMMETRICAL PANDIAGONAL PERFECT MAGIC CUBE

23	240	566	472	308	655	837	784	111
764	171	3	250	536	482	318	625	847
605	857	734	181	13	220	546	462	378
432	388	615	827	744	161	73	200	556
210	526	442	368	675	807	754	131	83
141	63	270	506	452	338	685	817	724
877	704	151	33	280	516	422	348	665
358	635	887	714	121	43	260	576	402
586	412	328	645	867	774	101	53	230

R = 8

FIGURE 8–7. TOP ORTHOGONAL SECTION

23	764	605	432	210	141	877	358	586
305	532	10	741	677	458	286	123	864
110	841	377	558	86	723	664	405	232
477	258	186	823	364	505	32	710	641
786	623	464	205	132	810	341	577	58
564	5	732	610	441	277	158	886	323
832	310	541	77	758	686	423	264	105
241	177	858	386	523	64	705	632	410
658	486	223	164	805	332	510	41	777

C = 0

FIGURE 8–8. LEFT SIDE ORTHOGONAL SECTION

658	835	787	114	21	243	560	476	302
177	4	251	533	480	316	622	848	765
541	463	370	606	852	738	185	17	224
610	826	742	168	75	207	554	431	383
132	88	215	527	444	361	673	800	756
505	457	334	681	813	720	146	62	278
664	871	703	150	36	282	518	425	347
123	40	266	572	408	355	637	884	711
586	412	328	645	867	774	101	53	230

777	104	51	233	580	416	322	648	865
632	888	715	127	44	261	573	400	356
423	340	666	872	708	155	37	284	511
277	504	451	333	680	816	722	148	65
132	88	215	527	444	361	673	800	756
823	740	166	72	208	555	437	384	611
377	604	851	733	180	16	222	548	465
532	488	315	627	844	761	173	0	256
23	240	566	472	308	655	837	784	111

FIGURE 8–9. DIAGONAL SECTIONS PERPENDICULAR TO LEFT SIDE
SHOWING SPACE DIAGONALS

Chapter 9

Odd-Order Magic Cubes

Thus far we have looked at several odd-order magic cubes (see Figure 9–1), but how about larger odd-order cubes? As you may have suspected, the answer is pandiagonal perfect magic cubes can be constructed for any odd-order cube where the order is nine or greater.

Order	Type of Cube That Can Be Constructed
3	Regular magic cube
5	Pandiagonal magic cube
7	Pandiagonal or perfect but not both at the same time
9	Pandiagonal perfect magic cube

Figure 9–1. Summary of Odd-Order Magic Cubes

Perpendicular to the side	a^2	b^2	$-ab$
Perpendicular to the top	b^2	$-ab$	a^2
Perpendicular to the front	$-ab$	a^2	b^2

Figure 9–2. Controlling Characteristics of the Orthogonals for Case 5

To show this let us consider as Case 5 a very general cube (see Figure 9–2), namely (where a is not equal to b),

$$\begin{vmatrix} a & b & 0 \\ b & 0 & a \\ 0 & a & b \end{vmatrix}_N \quad \Delta = a^3 + b^3$$

Thus for Case 5:

(a) The value of Δ is $a^3 + b^3$,
(b) The controlling characteristics for the diagonals in the orthogonal sections equal $a^2 \pm b^2$, $a^2 \pm ab$, and $b^2 \pm ab$, and
(c) The controlling characteristics for the space diagonals equal $a^2 \pm ab \pm b^2$.

CASE		Δ	CONTROLLING CHARACTERISTICS		
			Orthogonals	Diagonals	Space Diagonals
3	a = 1, b = 2	9	1, 2, 4	1, 2, 3, 5, 6	1, 3, 5, 7
4	a = 1, b = −2	−7	1, 2, 4	1, 2, 3, 5, 6	1, 3, 5, 7
5	a = 1, b = −24	−23 × 601	1, 24, 576	23, 25, 552, 575, 577, 600	551, 553, 599, 601
6	a = 1, b = 100	101 × 9,901	1, 100, 10,000	99, 101, 9,900, 9,999, 10,001, 10,100	9,899, 9,901, 10,099, 10,101

FIGURE 9–3. SUMMARY OF CASES

Note the following for the cases summarized in Figure 9–3:

Case 3 may be used for any odd N above 9 where N is prime to 3 because then N will be prime to Δ and none of the controlling characteristics are a multiple of N—all are smaller than N. Note that it makes no difference if N and a controlling characteristic have a common factor. Common factors can be taken care of when assigning values to the letters in the orthogonal or diagonal involved.

Case 4 may be used for any odd N above 7 where N is prime to 7 because then N will be prime to Δ and none of the controlling characteristics are a multiple of N—all are smaller than N.

Case 5 may be used for any N above 7 when N is not prime to both 3 and 7 (that is, when $N = 21k$, where k is a positive integer) but is prime to both 23 and 601, inasmuch as N will be prime to Δ and none of the controlling characteristics are a multiple of 21 and hence cannot be a multiple of $N = 21k$.

Case 6 may be used for any odd N where N is not prime to 3, 7, and 23 (that is, when $N = 3 \times 7 \times 23 \times j = 483j$, where j is a positive integer) or to 3, 7, and 601 (that is, when $N = 3 \times 7 \times 601 \times m = 12,621m$, where m is a positive integer) but is prime to 101 and 9,901, inasmuch as N will be prime to Δ and none of the controlling characteristics are a multiple of 483 or 12,621 and hence cannot be a multiple of $N = 483j$ or of $N = 12,621m$.

Notice that we have covered

(a)   with Cases 3 or 4 all odd N up to 21 and, also, all odd N where N is a prime number greater than 7;

(b)   with cases 3, 4, or 5, all odd N up to $3 \times 7 \times 23 = 483$; and

(c)   with cases 3, 4, 5, or 6, all odd N up to $3 \times 7 \times 23 \times 101 = 48,783$.

While the above is not a mathematical proof for *all* odd N, we are sure that our readers will agree that it does cover all cases, where N is odd, that are of any practical interest.

Chapter 10

Singly-Even Magic Cubes

Singly-even magic cubes (cubes of order N, where N is divisible by 2 but not by 4) like singly-even magic squares, present special difficulties. J. Barkley Rosser and Robert J. Walker proved in the late 1930s that pandiagonal perfect magic cubes of order $N = 2m$, where m is an odd number, cannot exist.[1]

Simple $6 \times 6 \times 6$ magic cubes have been known for some time. The reference to the earliest sixth-order cube that we have seen is to one constructed by W. Firth, Scholar of Emmanuel, Cambridge, England, in 1889.[2] In *Magic Squares and Cubes* W. S. Andrews presents two different ways of constructing such cubes, but they are not easy to follow.[3] In the same book Dr. C. Planck presents an excellent discussion of how to construct magic squares and cubes by means of "Reversions."[4] (It was an extension of this method that we employed in Chapter 6 for the construction of the first perfect $8 \times 8 \times 8$ magic cube. Planck limited himself to the discussion of simple magic cubes.) Planck extended his method ingeniously to sixth-order magic cubes.

It is not to show that such cubes can be constructed by various methods but to demonstrate the extreme flexibility of the

1. J. Barkley Rosser and Robert J. Walker, "The Algebraic Theory of Diabolic Magic Squares: Supplement," (Ithaca, New York: Cornell University Library, n.d.), pp. 740–741.
2. Cited by Dr. C. Planck, "The Theory of Reversions," in W. S. Andrews, *Magic Squares and Cubes: With Chapters by Other Writers,* 2nd ed. rev. (1917; reprint ed., New York: Dover Publications, 1960), pp. 298, 304–305.
3. Andrews, ibid.
4. C. Planck, "The Theory of Reversions," in ibid., pp. 295–320.

cyclical method (when combined with an intermediate cube) that we will now use the latter method to construct a sixth-order magic cube. We shall use a slight modification of Case 4, which we shall designate as Case 7:

$$\begin{vmatrix} 2 & 1 & 0 \\ 1 & 0 & 2 \\ 0 & -2 & 1 \end{vmatrix}_N \quad \Delta = 7$$

	x	X	x
Perpendicular to the side	−4	1	−2
Perpendicular to the top	1	−2	4
Perpendicular to the front	2	−4	1

FIGURE 10–1. CONTROLLING CHARACTERISTICS OF THE ORTHOGONALS

The controlling characteristics for the diagonals in the orthogonal sections are (as in Cases 3 and 4) 1, 2, 3, 5, and 6 (see Figure 10–1). The controlling characteristics for the space diagonals (again, as in Cases 3 and 4) are 1, 3, 5, and 7. Let us now use our standard procedure and the generating characteristics of Case 7 to construct the six orthogonal sections parallel to the front and the two diagonal sections perpendicular to the left side and check them against our expected results to see what requirements we must meet for the cube to be magic (see Figures 10–2, 10–3).

Ignoring for the moment the lines indicating transfers, if we make no interchanges (or if we do make one, we also make a counteracting one) in the numbers occupying the space diagonals, the italic letters will, in three of the four cases, be automatically magic and, in the fourth case, will be magic if we make $a + d = 5$. The same situation exists for the capital letters—three of the diagonals are automatically correct and the fourth requires that $C + F = 5$. For the lowercase letters the fourth diagonal requires that $b + e = 5$. To summarize, if the following conditions are met the space diagonals will be magic:

(a) $a + d = C + F = b + e = 5$ (which is easy to meet), and
(b) If any interchange of the numbers lying in the cells on the

space diagonals is made, a second interchange will be made that will have a compensating effect.

Looking now at the various orthogonals (we can readily see that the situation with the diagonals in the orthogonal sections is hopeless), note that the italic letters require that $a+c+e=b+d+f$. Similarly, the capital letters require that $A+C+E=B+D+F$. The lowercase letters require that $a+c+e=b+d+f$.

It is when we try to meet this condition that we first strike trouble. The sum of the numbers 0, 1, 2, 3, 4, and 5 is 15 and there is no way that we can divide 15 into two equal parts. The

eEb°	aDf	cCd	eBb	aAf	cFd
cCc	eBa	aAe	cFc	eEa°	aDe
aAd	cFb	eEf	aDd	cCb	eBf°
eEe	aDc	cCa°	eBe	aAc	cFa
cCf	eBd	aAb	cFf°	eEd	aDb
aAa	cFe°	eEc	aDa	cCe	eBc

Front D = 0

dCf	fBd	bAb°	dFf	fEd	bDb
bAa°	dFe	fEc	bDa	dCe	fBc
fEb	bDf°	dCd	fBb	bAf	dFd
dCc	fBa	bAe	dFc	fEa°	bDe
bAd	dFb	fEf	bDd	dCb	fBf°
fEe	bDc	dCa	fBe°	bAc	dFa

D = 1

cAd	eFb	aEf	cDd	eCb°	aBf
aEe	cDc	eCa°	aBe	cAc°	eFa
eCf	aBd	cAb	eFf°	aEd	cDb
cAa°	eFe	aEc	cDa	eCe	aBc
aEb	cDf°	eCd	aBb	cAf	eFd
eCc	aBa	cAe	eFc	aEa	cDe°

D = 2

bEb°	dDf	fCd	bBb	dAf	fFd
fCc	bBa°	dAe	fFc	bEa°	dDe
dAd	fFb	bEf	dDd	fCb	bBf°
bEe	dDc	fCa°	bBe	dAc	fFa
fCf	bBd	dAb	fFf°	bEd	dDb
dAa	fFe°	bEc	dDa	fCe	bBc

D = 3

aCf	cBd	eAb°	aFf	cEd	eDb
eAa°	aFe	cEc	eDa	aCe	cBc
cEb	eDf°	aCd	cBb	eAf	aFd
aCc	cBa	eAe	aFc	cEa°	eDe
eAd	aFb	cEf	eDd	aCb	cBf°
cEe	eDc	aCa	cBe°	eAc	aFa

D = 4

fAd	bFb	dEf	fDd	bCb°	dBf
dEc	fDc	bCa°	dBe	fAc	bFa
bCf	dBd	fAb	bFf°	dEd	fDb
fAa°	bFe	dEc	fDa	bCe	dBc
dEb	fDf°	bCd	dBb	fAf	bFd
bCc	dBa	fAe	bFc	dEa	fDe°

Back D = 5

FIGURE 10–2. ORTHOGONAL SECTIONS PARALLEL TO THE FRONT

Low back   High back

bCc	dBa	fAe	bFc	dEa	fDe°
eAd	aFb	cEf	eDd	aCb	cBf°
bEe	dDc	fCa°	bBe	dAc	fFa
eCf	aBd	cAb	eFf°	aEd	cDb
bAa°	dFe	fEc	bDa	dCe	fBc
eEb°	aDf	cCd	eBb	aAf	cFd

fAd	bFb	dEf	fDd	bCb°	dBf
eAa°	aFe	cEc	eDa	aCe	cBc
dAd	fFb	bEf	dDd	fCb	bBf°
cAa°	eFe	aEc	cDa	eCe	aBc
bAd	dFb	fEf	bDd	dCb	fBf°
aAa	cFe°	eEc	aDa	cCe	eBc

High front   Low front

FIGURE 10–3. SPACE DIAGONAL SECTIONS PERPENDICULAR TO LEFT SIDE

best we can do is to let, say, $a + c + e = 8$ and $b + d + f = 7$ and see if we can do this and still have the letters so assigned that it is possible to interchange numbers between cells and make the totals correct—part of the technique we used with singly-even magic squares. This is not easy, but it is possible.

We shall examine the situation with respect to the lowercase letters first. Look at cCc in cell [0,4,0] and cCf in cell [0,1,0]. If we interchange these two numbers we will make no change in the italic or capital letters (they are the same for both numbers), but we will make the letters in two of the orthogonals through cell [0,4,0] (the orthogonal perpendicular to the left side and the one perpendicular to the front) equal to $2(a + c + e) + (f - c)$. These letters will have the correct sum, 15, if $(a + c + e) = 8$ and $(f - c) = -1$. It will also (without making any change in the italic and capital letters involved) make the letters in two of the orthogonals through cell [0,1,0] (again the orthogonal perpendicular to the left side and the one perpendicular to the front) equal to $2(b + d + f) + (c - f)$. These also will sum to the correct amount, 15, if $(b + d + f) = 7$ and $(c - f) = 1$. Note that this interchange had no affect on the letters forming the third orthogonal through these two cells—the one common to them both (perpendicular to the top), which, since it contained each letter once and only once, was correct before any interchanges were made. Now let us look at fBa in cell [1,2,1] and fBd in cell [1,5,1]. If this interchange is made we will correct the sum of the lowercase letters in the two orthogonals perpendicular to the left side and the two perpendicular to the front that pass through these two cells without affecting the third orthogonal passing through them provided we can make

$$2(a+c+e)=16, \qquad (d-a)=-1, \qquad \text{and}$$

$$2(b+d+f)=14, \qquad (a-d)=1.$$

If we let $a=5$, $c=1$, $e=2$, $b=3$, $d=4$, and $f=0$, we are able to meet all of the necessary requirements to make the interchanges work. Can we make all of the necessary interchanges without interchanging any number we have interchanged before? Can we space the interchanges so that we have made one interchange affecting every orthogonal perpendicular to the left side once, and only once, and at the same time made similar corrections to the orthogonals perpendicular to the front?

Difficult as they are, the interchanges can be made, as the vertical transfer lines in Figure 10–2 show. Notice that the three vertical interchanges on any one of the orthogonal sections parallel to the front correct all orthogonals lying on that section that are perpendicular to the left side. Check the orthogonals in column 0 in sections $D=0$, $D=2$, and $D=4$. Here you will see that the vertical interchanges correct all orthogonals perpendicular to the front in the orthogonal section $C=0$. All of the orthogonals parallel to these are also corrected as required.

The capital letters have the following requirements:

$$2(A+C+E)=16 \qquad (A-D)=(E-B)=1$$

$$2(B+D+F)=14 \qquad (D-A)=(B-E)=-1$$

and, of course, as we saw earlier, $(C+F)=5$. The italic letters require that

$$2(a+c+e)=16 \qquad (c-f)=(e-b)=1$$

$$2(b+d+f)=14 \qquad (f-c)=(b-e)=-1$$

and $(a+d)=5$. All that is needed to meet these requirements is to let $A=5$, $C=2$, $E=1$, $B=0$, $D=4$, $F=3$, $a=2$, $c=1$, $e=5$, $b=4$, $d=3$, and $f=0$.

Substituting these values and making the indicated interchanges will give you the six orthogonal sections parallel to the front (see Figure 10–4), the two diagonal sections perpendicular to the left side (Figure 10–5), the six orthogonal sections parallel to the top (Figure 10–6), and the six orthogonal sections parallel to the left side (Figure 10–7).

413	240	124	503	251	134
120	505	252	131	415	242
254	133	511	244	123	400
512	241	25	502	250	135
121	514	243	30	504	253
245	32	510	255	122	501

Front D = 0

320	5	553	330	14	443
555	332	1	444	322	11
3	540	324	13	450	335
321	4	452	331	115	442
454	333	10	445	323	100
12	451	325	102 `	441	334

D = 1

144	533	211	154	423	200
212	141	425	202	150	535
521	214	143	430	204	153
55	532	210	145	522	201
213	40	524	203	151	534
520	205	152	531	215	42

D = 2

513	340	24	403	350	35
21	404	352	31	515	342
354	33	410	345	23	500
402	351	125	412	341	34
20	405	353	130	414	343
355	132	401	344	22	411

D = 3

221	114	453	230	104	543
455	232	110	545	222	101
113	440	224	103	551	234
220	105	542	231	15	552
544	233	111	554	223	0
112	541	225	2	550	235

D = 4

54	433	300	45	523	310
302	51	525	312	41	434
420	305	53	530	314	43
155	432	311	44	422	301
313	140	424	303	50	435
421	304	52	431	315	142

Back D = 5

FIGURE 10–4. ORTHOGONAL SECTIONS PARALLEL TO THE FRONT

Low Back

421	304	52	431	315	142
544	233	111	554	223	0
402	351	125	412	341	34
521	214	143	430	204	153
555	332	1	444	322	11
413	240	124	503	251	134

High front

High Back

54	433	300	45	523	310
455	232	110	545	222	101
354	33	410	345	23	500
55	532	210	145	522	201
454	333	10	445	323	100
245	32	510	255	122	501

Low Front

FIGURE 10–5. SPACE DIAGONAL SECTIONS PERPENDICULAR TO LEFT SIDE

421	304	52	431	315	142
112	541	225	2	550	235
355	132	401	344	22	411
520	205	152	531	215	42
12	451	325	102	441	334
245	32	510	255	122	501

Bottom R = 0

313	140	424	303	50	435
544	233	111	554	223	0
20	405	353	130	414	343
213	40	524	203	151	534
454	333	10	445	323	100
121	514	243	030	504	253

R = 1

155	432	311	44	422	301
220	105	542	231	15	552
402	351	125	412	341	34
55	532	210	145	522	201
321	4	452	331	115	442
512	241	25	502	250	135

R = 2

420	305	53	530	314	43
113	440	224	103	551	234
354	33	410	345	23	500
521	214	143	430	204	153
3	540	324	13	450	335
254	133	511	244	123	400

R = 3

302	51	525	312	41	434
455	232	110	545	222	101
21	404	352	31	515	342
212	141	425	202	150	535
555	332	1	444	322	11
120	505	252	131	415	242

R = 4

54	433	300	45	523	310
221	114	453	230	104	543
513	340	24	403	350	35
144	533	211	154	423	200
320	5	553	330	14	443
413	240	124	503	251	134

Top R = 5

FIGURE 10–6. ORTHOGONAL SECTIONS PARALLEL TO THE TOP

54	221	513	144	320	413
302	455	21	212	555	120
420	113	354	521	3	254
155	220	402	55	321	512
313	544	20	213	454	121
421	112	355	520	12	245

Left side C = 0

433	114	340	533	5	240
51	232	404	141	332	505
305	440	33	214	540	133
432	105	351	532	4	241
140	233	405	40	333	514
304	541	132	205	451	32

C = 1

300	453	24	211	553	124
525	110	352	425	1	252
53	224	410	143	324	511
311	542	125	210	452	25
424	111	353	524	10	243
52	225	401	152	325	510

C = 2

45	230	403	154	330	503
312	545	31	202	444	131
530	103	345	430	13	244
44	231	412	145	331	502
303	554	130	203	445	30
431	2	344	531	102	255

C = 3

523	104	350	423	14	251
41	222	515	150	322	415
314	551	23	204	450	123
422	15	341	522	115	250
50	223	414	151	323	504
315	550	22	215	441	122

C = 4

310	543	35	200	443	134
434	101	342	535	11	242
43	234	500	153	335	400
301	552	34	201	442	135
435	0	343	534	100	253
142	235	411	42	334	501

Right side C = 5

FIGURE 10–7. ORTHOGONAL SECTIONS PARALLEL TO LEFT SIDE

Notice that the horizontal interchanges in the orthogonal sections parallel to the front make the necessary corrections to the capital letters and that those indicated by the small degree mark (°) indicate the interchanges between numbers in planes $D = 0$ and $D = 3$, which lie on the orthogonals perpendicular to the front of the cube. The interchanges between planes $D = 1$

and $D=4$ and between planes $D=2$ and $D=5$ are similarly marked.

Now let us turn our attention to the construction of a $10 \times 10 \times 10$ pandiagonal magic cube. Consider the cube $N = 2(2m + 1)$ and generate the original intermediate cube using

$$\begin{vmatrix} \pm 1 & 2m & 0 \\ 2m & 0 & \pm 1 \\ 0 & \pm 1 & 2m \end{vmatrix}_N \qquad \Delta = 8m^3 \pm 1$$

Note that when we use the plus sign before 1 that $\Delta = 8m^3 + 1$ and that when we use the minus sign $\Delta = 8m^3 - 1$. Hence the proper selection of sign will enable us to select a Δ which will, for all practical values of N, be prime to N, as required.

The orthogonal characteristics of this cube will be 1, 2m, and $4m^2$. It follows that, while the main diagonals cannot be made magic, the space diagonals' characteristics will be $1 + 2m + 4m^2$, $-1 + 2m + 4m^2$, $1 - 2m + 4m^2$, and $-1 - 2m + 4m^2$. Noting that

$$2m + 4m^2 = 2m(2m + 1) = 0 \bmod N$$

and that

$$-2m + 4m^2 = -4m = +2 \bmod N$$

we have orthogonal characteristics equal to 1, 2m, and $-2m$, and space diagonal characteristics equal to 1 and 3.

For $m = 2$ this gives us the following generating characteristics for a $10 \times 10 \times 10$ cube, which we shall designate as Case 8:

$$\begin{vmatrix} -1 & 4 & 0 \\ 4 & 0 & -1 \\ 0 & -1 & 4 \end{vmatrix}_N \qquad \Delta = 63$$

The orthogonal characteristics are equal to 1 and 4; the space diagonal characteristics are equal to 1 and 3. We therefore expect to find the letters appearing once and only once whenever the characteristics are 1 and 3 and twice when the characteristic is 4. The orthogonal sections parallel to the front of the cube and the diagonal sections perpendicular to the left side show that this is the case (see Figures 10–8 through 10–21).

Note that when the orthogonals consist of five different letters, each repeated twice, they appear as A, C, E, G, and I, or B, D, F, H, and J. Also note that the space diagonals, including the broken space diagonals, are all automatically correct—as is necessary if the cube is to be a pandiagonal magic cube.

dCi	bEf	jGc	hIj	fAg	dCd	bEa	jGh	hIe	fAb°
gEg	eGd	cIa	aAh	iCe	gEb	eGi	cIf	aAc°	iCj
jGe	hIb	fAi	dCf	bEc	jGj	hIg	fAd°	dCa	bEh
cIc	aAj	iCg	gEd	eGa	cIh	aAe°	iCb	gEi	eGf
fAa	dCh	bEe	jGb	hIi	fAf°	dCc	bEj	jGg	hId
iCi	gEf	eGc	cIj	aAg°	iCd	gEa	eGh	cIe	aAb
bEg	jGd	hIa	fAh°	dCe	bEb	jGi	hIf	fAc	dCj
eGe	cIb	aAi°	iCf	gEc	eGj	cIg	aAd	iCa	gEh
hIc	fAj°	dCg	bEd	jGa	hIh	fAe	dCb	bEi	jGf
aAa°	iCh	gEe	eGb	cIi	aAf	iCc	gEj	eGg	cId

FIGURE 10–8. FRONT ORTHOGONAL SECTION

fJg	dBd	bDa	jFh	hHe	fJb	dBi	bDf	jFc°	hHj
iBe	gDb	eFi	cHf	aJc	iBj	gDg	eFd°	cHa	aJh
bDc	jFj	hHg	fJd	dBa	bDh	jFe°	hHb	fJi	dBf
eFa	cHh	aJe	iBb	gDi	eFf°	cHc	aJj	iBg	gDd
hHi	fJf	dBc	bDj	jFg°	hHd	fJa	dBh	bDe	jFb
aJg	iBd	gDa	eFh°	cHe	aJb	iBi	gDf	eFc	cHj
dBe	bDb	jFi°	hHf	fJc	dBj	bDg	jFd	hHa	fJh
gDc	eFj°	cHg	aJd	iBa	gDh	eFe	cHb	aJi	iBf
jFa°	hHh	fJe	dBb	bDi	jFf	hHc	fJj	dBg	bDd
cHi	aJf	iBc	gDj	eFg	cHd	aJa	iBh	gDe	eFb°

D = 1

FIGURE 10–9. SECOND ORTHOGONAL SECTION

hGe	fIb	dAi	bCf	jEc	hGj	fIg	dAd°	bCa	jEh
aIc	iAj	gCg	eEd	cGa	aIh	iAe°	gCb	eEi	cGf
dAa	bCh	jEe	hGb	fIi	dAf°	bCc	jEj	hGg	fId
gCi	eEf	cGc	aIj	iAg°	gCd	eEa	cGh	aIe	iAb
jEg	hGd	fIa	dAh°	bCe	jEb	hGi	fIf	dAc	bCj
cGe	aIb	iAi°	gCf	eEc	cGj	aIg	iAd	gCa	eEh
fIc	dAj°	bCg	jEd	hGa	fIh	dAe	bCb	jEi	hGf
iAa°	gCh	eEe	cGb	aIi	iAf	gCc	eEj	cGg	aId
bCi	jEf	hGc	fIj	dAg	bCd	jEa	hGh	fIe	dAb°
eEg	cGd	aIa	iAh	gCe	eEb	cGi	aIf	iAc°	gCj

D = 2

FIGURE 10–10. THIRD ORTHOGONAL SECTION

jDc	hFj	fHg	dJd	bBa	jDh	hFe°	fHb	dJi	bBf
cFa	aHh	iJe	gBb	eDi	cFf°	aHc	iJj	gBg	eDd
fHi	dJf	bBc	jDj	hFg°	fHd	dJa	bBh	jDe	hFb
iJg	gBd	eDa	cFh°	aHe	iJb	gBi	eDf	cFc	aHj
bBe	jDb	hFi°	fHf	dJc	bBj	jDg	hFd	fHa	dJh
eDc	cFj°	aHg	iJd	gBa	eDh	cFe	aHb	iJi	gBf
hFa°	fHh	dJe	bBb	jDi	hFf	fHc	dJj	bBg	jDd
aHi	iJf	gBc	eDj	cFg	aHd	iJa	gBh	eDe	cFb°
dJg	bBd	jDa	hFh	fHe	dJb	bBi	jDf	hFc°	fHj
gBe	eDb	cFi	aHf	iJc	gBj	eDg	cFd°	aHa	iJh

D = 3

FIGURE 10–11. FOURTH ORTHOGONAL SECTION

bAa	jCh	hEe	fGb	dIi	bAf°	jCc	hEj	fGg	dId
eCi	cEf	aGc	iIj	gAg°	eCd	cEa	aGh	iIe	gAb
hEg	fGd	dIa	bAh°	jCe	hEb	fGi	dIf	bAc	jCj
aGe	iIb	gAi°	eCf	cEc	aGj	iIg	gAd	eCa	cEh
dIc	bAj°	jCg	hEd	fGa	dIh	bAe	jCb	hEi	fGf
gAa°	eCh	cEe	aGb	iIi	gAf	eCc	cEj	aGg	iId
jCi	hEf	fGc	dIj	bAg	jCd	hEa	fGh	dIe	bAb°
cEg	aGd	iIa	gAh	eCe	cEb	aGi	iIf	gAc°	eCj
fGe	dIb	bAi	jCf	hEc	fGj	dIg	bAd°	jCa	hEh
iIc	gAj	eCg	cEd	aGa	iIh	gAe°	eCb	cEi	aGf

D = 4

FIGURE 10–12. FIFTH ORTHOGONAL SECTION

dHi	bJf	jBc	hDj	fFg	dHd	bJa	jBh	hDe	fFb°
gJg	eBd	cDa	aFh	iHe	gJb	eBi	cDf	aFc°	iHj
jBe	hDb	fFi	dHf	bJc	jBj	hDg	fFd°	dHa	bJh
cDc	aFj	iHg	gJd	eBa	cDh	aFe°	iHb	gJi	eBf
fFa	dHh	bJe	jBb	hDi	fFf°	dHc	bJj	jBg	hDd
iHi	gJf	eBc	cDj	aFg°	iHd	gJa	eBh	cDe	aFb
bJg	jBd	hDa	fFh°	dHe	bJb	jBi	hDf	fFc	dHj
eBe	cDb	aFi°	iHf	gJc	eBj	cDg	aFd	iHa	gJh
hDc	fFj°	dHg	bJd	jBa	hDh	fFe	dHb	bJi	jBf
aFa°	iHh	gJe	eBb	cDi	aFf	iHc	gJj	eBg	cDd

D = 5

FIGURE 10–13. SIXTH ORTHOGONAL SECTION

fEg	dGd	bIa	jAh	hCe	fEb	dGi	bIf	jAc°	hCj
iGe	gIb	eAi	cCf	aEc	iGj	gIg	eAd°	cCa	aEh
bIc	jAj	hCg	fEd	dGa	bIh	jAe°	hCb	fEi	dGf
eAa	cCh	aEe	iGb	gIi	eAf°	cCc	aEj	iGg	gId
hCi	fEf	dGc	bIj	jAg°	hCd	fEa	dGh	bIe	jAb
aEg	iGd	gIa	eAh°	cCe	aEb	iGi	gIf	eAc	cCj
dGe	bIb	jAi°	hCf	fEc	dGj	bIg	jAd	hCa	fEh
gIc	eAj°	cCg	aEd	iGa	gIh	eAe	cCb	aEi	iGf
jAa°	hCh	fEe	dGb	bIi	jAf	hCc	fEj	dGg	bId
cCi	aEf	iGc	gIj	eAg	cCd	aEa	iGh	gIe	eAb°

D = 6

FIGURE 10–14. SEVENTH ORTHOGONAL SECTION

hBe	fDb	dFi	bHf	jJc	hBj	fDg	dFd°	bHa	jJh
aDc	iFj	gHg	eJd	cBa	aDh	iFe°	gHb	eJi	cBf
dFa	bHh	jJe	hBb	fDi	dFf°	bHc	jJj	hBg	fDd
gHi	eJf	cBc	aDj	iFg°	gHd	eJa	cBh	aDe	iFb
jJg	hBd	fDa	dFh°	bHe	jJb	hBi	fDf	dFc	bHj
cBe	aDb	iFi°	gHf	eJc	cBj	aDg	iFd	gHa	eJh
fDc	dFj°	bHg	jJd	hBa	fDh	dFe	bHb	jJi	hBf
iFa°	gHh	eJe	cBb	aDi	iFf	gHc	eJj	cBg	aDd
bHi	jJf	hBc	fDj	dFg	bHd	jJa	hBh	fDe	dFb°
eJg	cBd	aDa	iFh	gHe	eJb	cBi	aDf	iFc°	gHj

D = 7

FIGURE 10–15. EIGHTH ORTHOGONAL SECTION

jIc	hAj	fCg	dEd	bGa	jIh	hAe°	fCb	dEi	bGf
cAa	aCh	iEe	gGb	eIi	cAf°	aCc	iEj	gGg	eId
fCi	dEf	bGc	jIj	hAg°	fCd	dEa	bGh	jIe	hAb
iEg	gGd	eIa	cAh°	aCe	iEb	gGi	eIf	cAc	aCj
bGe	jIb	hAi°	fCf	dEc	bGj	jIg	hAd	fCa	dEh
eIc	cAj°	aCg	iEd	gGa	eIh	cAe	aCb	iEi	gGf
hAa°	fCh	dEe	bGb	jIi	hAf	fCc	dEj	bGg	jId
aCi	iEf	gGc	eIj	cAg	aCd	iEa	gGh	eIe	cAb°
dEg	bGd	jIa	hAh	fCe	dEb	bGi	jIf	hAc°	fCj
gGe	eIb	cAi	aCf	iEc	gGj	eIg	cAd°	aCa	iEh

D = 8

FIGURE 10–16. NINTH ORTHOGONAL SECTION

bFa	jHh	hJe	fBb	dDi	bFf°	jHc	hJj	fBg	dDd
eHi	cJf	aBc	iDj	gFg°	eHd	cJa	aBh	iDe	gFb
hJg	fBd	dDa	bFh°	jHe	hJb	fBi	dDf	bFc	jHj
aBe	iDb	gFi°	eHf	cJc	aBj	iDg	gFd	eHa	cJh
dDc	bFj°	jHg	hJd	fBa	dDh	bFe	jHb	hJi	fBf
gFa°	eHh	cJe	aBb	iDi	gFf	eHc	cJj	aBg	iDd
jHi	hJf	fBc	dDj	bFg	jHd	hJa	fBh	dDe	bFb°
cJg	aBd	iDa	gFh	eHe	cJb	aBi	iDf	gFc°	eHj
fBe	dDb	bFi	jHf	hJc	fBj	dDg	bFd°	jHa	hJh
iDc	gFj	eHg	cJd	aBa	iDh	gFe°	eHb	cJi	aBf

D = 9

FIGURE 10–17. TENTH ORTHOGONAL SECTION

dCi	bEf	jGc	hIj	fAg	dCd	bEa	jGh	hIe	fAb°
iBe	gDb	eFi	cHf	aJc	iBj	gDg	eFd°	cHa	aJh
dAa	bCh	jEe	hGb	fIi	dAf°	bCc	jEj	hGg	fId
iJg	gBd	eDa	cFh°	aHe	iJb	gBi	eDf	cFc	aHj
dIc	bAj°	jCg	hEd	fGa	dIh	bAe	jCb	hEi	fGf
iHi	gJf	eBc	cDj	aFg°	iHd	gJa	eBh	cDe	aFb
dGe	bIb	jAi°	hCf	fEc	dGj	bIg	jAd	hCa	fEh
iFa°	gHh	eJe	cBb	aDi	iFf	gHc	eJj	cBg	aDd
dEg	bGd	jIa	hAh	fCe	dEb	bGi	jIf	hAc°	fCj
iDc	gFj	eHg	cJd	aBa	iDh	gFe°	eHb	cJi	aBf

FIGURE 10–18. DIAGONAL SECTION PERPENDICULAR TO LEFT SIDE SHOWING SPACE DIAGONALS BEFORE ANY INTERCHANGES

bFa	jHh	hJe	fBb	dDi	bFf°	jHc	hJj	fBg	dDd
cAa	aCh	iEe	gGb	eIi	cAf°	aCc	iEj	gGg	eId
dFa	bHh	jJe	hBb	fDi	dFf°	bHc	jJj	hBg	fDd
eAa	cCh	aEe	iGb	gIi	eAf°	cCc	aEj	iGg	gId
fFa	dHh	bJe	jBb	hDi	fFf°	dHc	bJj	jBg	hDd
gAa°	eCh	cEe	aGb	iIi	gAf	eCc	cEj	aGg	iId
hFa°	fHh	dJe	bBb	jDi	hFf	fHc	dJj	bBg	jDd
iAa°	gCh	eEe	cGb	aIi	iAf	gCc	eEj	cGg	aId
jFa°	hHh	fJe	dBb	bDi	jFf	hHc	fJj	dBg	bDd
aAa°	iCh	gEe	eGb	cIi	aAf	iCc	gEj	eGg	cId

FIGURE 10–19. DIAGONAL SECTION PERPENDICULAR TO LEFT SIDE SHOWING THE OTHER SPACE DIAGONALS BEFORE ANY INTERCHANGES

dCi	gEf	jGc	hIj	fAg	dCd	bEa	jGh	hIe	fFb
iBe	gDb	eFi	hHf	aJc	iBj	gDg	eAd	cHa	aJh
dAa	gCh	jEe	hGb	fIi	dFf	bCc	jEj	hGg	fId
iJg	gBi	jDa	cAh	aHe	iJb	gBd	eDf	cFc	aHj
dIc	bFj	eCg	hEi	fGa	dIh	bAe	jCb	hEd	fGf
iHi	gJf	eBc	cDj	aAg	iHd	bJa	eBh	cDe	aFb
dGe	bIb	jFi	hCf	fEc	dGj	bIg	jAd	cCa	fEh
iAa	gHh	eJe	cBb	aDi	iFf	bHc	eJj	cBg	aDd
dEg	bGi	jIa	hAh	fCe	dEb	bGd	eIf	hFc	fCj
iDc	gFj	eHg	cJi	aBa	iDh	gAe	jHb	cJd	aBf

FIGURE 10–20. DIAGONAL SECTION PERPENDICULAR TO LEFT SIDE SHOWING SPACE DIAGONALS AFTER INTERCHANGES

bFa	jHh	hJe	fBb	dDi	bAf	jHc	cJj	fBg	dDd
cAa	aCh	iEe	gGb	eIi	cFf	aCc	iEj	gGg	jId
dFa	bHh	jJe	hBb	fDi	dAf	gHc	jJj	hBg	fDd
eAa	cCh	aEe	iGb	gIi	eFf	cCc	aEj	iGg	bId
fFa	dHh	bJe	jBb	hDi	fAf	dHc	bJj	jBg	cDd
gFa	eCh	hEe	aGb	iIi	gAf	eCc	cEj	aGg	iId
hAa	fHh	dJe	bBb	eDi	hFf	fHc	dJj	bBg	jDd
iFa	bCh	eEe	cGb	aIi	iAf	gCc	eEj	cGg	aId
jAa	hHh	fJe	dBb	gDi	jFf	hHc	fJj	dBg	bDd
aFa	iCh	gEe	eGb	hIi	aAf	iCc	gEj	eGg	cId

FIGURE 10–21. DIAGONAL SECTION PERPENDICULAR TO LEFT SIDE SHOWING THE OTHER DIAGONALS AFTER INTERCHANGES

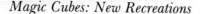

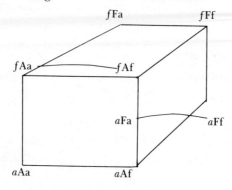

FIGURE 10–22. A 6 × 6 × 6 SUBCUBE

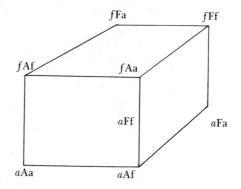

FIGURE 10–23. SWITCHING TWO CORNERS OF THE SUBCUBE

Our problem now is whether it is possible to correct the orthogonals where five different letters each appear two times and not disturb the space diagonals, which are already correct.

Let us now examine the $6 \times 6 \times 6$ subcube which has the lower corner aAa (see Figure 10–22), and also the result of transposing fAa and fAf (the two numbers in the near upper edge) and aFa and aFf (the two numbers in the edge diagonally opposite the first two numbers that we transposed) (see Figure 10–23). We see that all twelve of the orthogonals forming the subcube contain the lowercase letters a and f rather than 2a or 2f. In other words, the orthogonals in the main cube will now consist of either all ten letters, each once and only once, or of $2(c+e+g+i)+a+f$. As we saw in the case of the $6 \times 6 \times 6$ cube, it is possible to assign values to these letters to make their sum correct.

Further examination of the subcube after the transfers will show that these interchanges had no affect on the space diagonals. We have made the double interchange of fAa and aFf with fAf and aFa, which clearly leaves the sums of the diagonals unchanged.

Therefore if every time we transpose two numbers to make it possible to correct the sum of the italic, capital, or lowercase letters in any given orthogonal, we also transpose the two numbers diagonally opposite them in the $6 \times 6 \times 6$ subcube containing the first two numbers, we will be able to correct all of the orthogonals involved without affecting the orthogonals or space diagonals that were correct originally.

The problem now reduces to: Can we make the necessary interchanges to correct all of the rows, columns, and files without interchanging any one number more than once? As shown by the indicated interchanges (horizontal lines for lowercase letters, vertical lines for italic letters, and ° for capital letters) in Figures 10–8 through 10–21, this very difficult deed can be done, provided we assign values to the letters so as to make

$$2(a+c+e+g+i)-c+h=2(b+d+f+h+i)-h+c$$

$$2(a+c+e+g+i)-e+j=2(b+d+f+h+j)-j+e$$

$$2(a+c+e+g+i)-g+b=2(b+d+f+h+j)-b+g$$

$$2(A+C+E+G+I)-A+F=2(B+D+F+H+J)-F+A$$

$$2(a+c+e+g+i)-c+h=2(b+d+f+h+j)-h+c$$

$$2(a+c+e+g+i)-i+d=2(b+d+f+h+j)-d+i$$

It is easy to see that this can be done in many different ways. For example,

$$a=1, \quad c=4, \quad e=8, \quad g=2, \quad i=7, \quad \text{and}$$

$$f=0, \quad h=5; \quad j=9, \quad b=3, \quad d=6$$

$$A=0, \quad C=5, \quad E=8, \quad G=2, \quad I=7, \quad \text{and}$$

$$F=1, \quad H=4, \quad J=9, \quad B=3, \quad D=6$$

$$a=1, \quad c=4, \quad e=9, \quad g=2, \quad i=6, \quad \text{and}$$

$$f=0, \quad h=5, \quad j=8, \quad b=3, \quad d=7$$

It only remains to make the indicated interchanges and to convert to the base 10 by adding 1 to 100 times the value corresponding to the italic letter, to 10 times the value corresponding to the capital letter, and to the value corresponding to the lowercase letter. We leave the actual completion of the cube to the interested reader, who will find no difficulty in completing it and in proving that it is indeed pandiagonally magic.

We believe this to be the first such cube ever to be constructed and are confident that the method can be extended to cover the construction of any larger singly-even pandiagonal magic cube provided that N is prime to 3. In fact we have constructed a singly-even $22 \times 22 \times 22$ pandiagonal magic cube. For singly-even perfect magic cubes see Chapter 12.

Chapter 11

Doubly-Even Magic Cubes

As far as difficulty is concerned, doubly-even cubes (those cubes where N is divisible by 4 but not by 8) fall somewhere between singly-even and triply-even cubes. J. Barkley Rosser and Robert J. Walker proved that pandiagonal perfect magic cubes of the order $N = 4m$, where m is an odd number, cannot exist.[1] We have already seen in the case of fourth-order magic cubes that pandiagonal magic cubes do exist. It is relatively simple to show that they also exist for any higher doubly-even order.

Let us consider as Case 9 another general cube:

$$\begin{vmatrix} 1 & 2m & 2m \\ 2m & 1 & 2m \\ 2m & 2m & 1 \end{vmatrix}_{N = 4m \text{ (m odd)}} \qquad \Delta = 1 \bmod N$$

	x	X	x
Perpendicular to the side	-1	2m	2m
Perpendicular to the top	2m	-1	2m
Perpendicular to the front	2m	2m	-1

FIGURE 11–1. CONTROLLING CHARACTERISTICS OF THE ORTHOGONALS

1. J. Barkley Rosser and Robert J. Walker, "The Algebraic Theory of Diabolic Magic Squares: Supplement," (Ithaca, New York: Cornell University Library, n.d.), pp. 740–741.

7579	492	4446	6282	2233	6879	1112	3526	4903	2613	7559	552	4426	6262	2173	6819	1052	3586	4923	2593
4425	6284	2231	6814	720	3585	4904	2611	7554	957	4445	6264	2171	6874	660	3525	4924	2591	7574	897
2223	6876	1118	3589	4907	2602	7556	558	4449	6267	2163	6816	1058	3529	4927	2582	7576	498	4429	6287
715	3597	4908	2601	7550	955	4460	6268	2161	6870	655	3537	4928	2581	7570	895	4440	6288	2221	6810
4912	2606	7543	553	4459	6272	2166	6802	1053	3599	4932	2586	7563	493	4439	6292	2226	6862	1113	3539
2606	951	4434	6280	2165	6804	651	3594	4937	2585	7564	891	4454	6300	2225	6864	711	3534	4917	2605
7544	6278	2169	6867	1043	3536	4938	2589	7567	482	4436	6298	2229	6807	1103	3596	4918	2609	7547	542
951	6808	1041	3530	4935	2600	7568	481	4430	6295	2237	6868	1101	3590	4915	2620	7548	541	4450	6275
4456	3522	4933	2599	7572	486	4423	6293	2239	6812	1106	3582	4913	2619	7552	546	4443	6273	2179	6872
6278	2594	7177	885	4424	6291	2234	7280	705	3524	4911	2614	7157	945	4444	6271	2174	7220	645	3584
2177	489	4447	6283	2236	6878	1109	3527	4902	2616	7558	549	4427	6263	2176	6818	1049	3587	4922	2596
6808	6281	2230	6815	717	3588	4901	2610	7555	960	4448	6261	2170	6875	657	3528	4921	2590	7575	900
1046	6873	1119	3592	4906	2603	7553	559	4452	6266	2162	6813	1059	3532	4926	2583	7573	499	4432	6286
3522	3600	4905	2604	7551	954	4457	6265	2164	6871	654	3540	4925	2584	7571	894	4437	6285	2224	6811
4931	2607	7542	556	4458	6269	2167	6803	1056	3598	4929	2587	7562	496	4438	6289	2227	6863	1116	3538
2594	950	4435	6277	2168	6801	650	3595	4940	2588	7561	890	4455	6297	2228	6861	710	3535	4920	2608
7578	6279	2172	6866	1042	3533	4939	2592	7566	483	4433	6299	2232	6806	1102	3593	4919	2612	7546	543
489	6805	1044	3531	4934	2597	7565	484	4431	6294	2240	6865	1104	3591	4914	2617	7545	544	4451	6274
6281	3523	4936	2598	7569	487	4422	6296	2238	6809	1107	3583	4916	2618	7549	547	4442	6276	2178	6869
4930	2595	7180	888	4421	6290	2235	7277	708	3521	4910	2615	7160	948	4441	6270	2175	7217	648	3581

D = 0

FIGURE 11–2. FRONT ORTHOGONAL SECTION OF A TWENTIETH-ORDER PERFECT MAGIC CUBE

There is no possibility of making the diagonals in the orthogonal sections magic, but, on the other hand, the space diagonals are automatically magic—they are 1 for every one of the four possible combinations of the controlling characteristics of the orthogonals (see Figure 11–1). Except for the labor involved when N is large, it is easy to construct a doubly-even-order pandiagonal magic cube of any given order using our cyclical method combined, as usual, with its intermediate cube.

1652	761	1601	800	1688	845	68	905	17	944	104	989
142	982	1678	723	34	915	1726	831	94	867	1611	771
84	817	121	936	1632	877	1668	961	1705	792	48	733
5	896	1640	857	113	956	1589	752	56	1001	1697	812
1647	766	15	946	1683	850	63	910	1599	802	99	994
133	984	1680	721	25	924	1717	840	96	865	1609	780
1664	821	125	932	1628	737	80	965	1709	788	44	881
10	891	1642	855	118	951	1594	747	58	999	1702	807
1656	757	13	948	1692	841	72	901	1597	804	108	985
1721	980	1676	725	29	776	137	836	92	869	1613	920
1659	819	123	934	1623	742	75	970	1707	790	46	886
1	900	60	997	109	960	1585	756	1644	853	1693	816

Front D = 0

1370	539	410	1223	1334	455	362	1259	1418	503	326	1175
292	1185	1348	573	400	1245	1300	465	340	1293	1408	525
1362	475	306	1231	1398	559	354	1195	1314	511	390	1279
431	1262	1391	434	323	1202	1439	542	383	1154	1331	482
1377	532	417	1216	1341	448	369	1252	1425	496	333	1168
295	1182	1351	571	403	1242	1303	462	342	1290	1411	522
1358	479	311	1235	1394	563	350	1199	1310	506	386	1283
424	1269	1384	441	316	1209	1432	549	376	1161	1324	489
1374	535	414	1218	1338	451	366	1255	1423	499	330	1171
299	1178	1346	566	407	1238	1307	458	347	1295	1415	518
1365	472	309	1228	1401	556	357	1192	1317	508	393	1276
427	1266	1387	438	319	1206	1435	546	379	1158	1327	486

D = 1

FIGURE 11–3 continued

1088	188	1133	212	1109	161	656	1484	701	1508	677	1457
711	1551	1059	154	603	1534	1011	262	663	1582	1042	202
660	252	697	1512	1045	1453	1092	1548	1129	216	613	157
581	1469	1064	281	692	1532	1013	173	632	1577	1124	236
1078	183	706	1515	1114	159	658	1479	1030	207	682	1563
577	1549	1068	277	612	1536	1009	253	636	1573	1044	240
1076	248	593	1520	1049	269	644	1544	1025	224	617	1565
579	1474	1095	286	687	1498	1143	178	627	1450	1119	238
1080	192	589	1524	1105	265	648	1488	1021	228	673	1561
1145	1553	1100	149	608	200	713	257	668	1445	1040	1496
1090	250	598	1503	1054	267	646	1539	1138	219	615	1455
709	1465	672	1441	696	1500	1141	169	1104	145	1128	204

D = 2

74	962	131	926	47	887	1658	818	1715	782	1631	743
1593	753	57	1000	1701	808	9	892	1641	856	112	952
1650	906	1603	798	103	847	66	762	19	942	1687	991
1727	839	86	875	1610	770	143	983	1670	731	26	914
76	969	1708	789	40	885	1660	825	124	933	1624	741
1501	751	54	1003	1698	810	7	895	1638	859	114	954
62	902	1607	794	107	995	1646	758	23	938	1691	851
1725	832	93	868	1617	772	141	976	1677	724	33	916
78	966	1711	786	43	883	1662	822	127	930	1627	739
11	755	50	1007	1694	950	1595	899	1634	863	110	806
64	904	1600	801	100	993	1648	765	16	945	1689	849
1723	835	1674	727	1614	774	139	979	90	871	30	918

D = 3

FIGURE 11–3   CONTINUED

356	1193	1316	509	392	1277	1364	473	308	1229	1400	557
1438	543	382	1155	1330	483	430	1263	1390	435	322	1203
372	1249	1428	493	336	1165	1380	529	420	1213	1344	445
1301	464	341	1292	1409	524	293	1184	1349	572	401	1244
351	1198	1311	514	387	1282	1359	478	303	1234	1395	562
1429	552	373	1153	1321	492	421	1272	1392	444	313	1212
368	1253	1421	497	332	1169	1376	533	416	1220	1340	449
1306	459	346	1287	1414	519	298	1179	1354	567	406	1239
360	1189	1320	516	396	1273	1368	469	301	1225	1404	553
1433	548	380	1160	1325	488	425	1268	1385	437	317	1208
363	1258	1419	502	327	1174	1371	538	411	1222	1335	454
1297	468	337	1296	1405	528	289	1188	1345	576	397	1248

D = 4

650	1547	707	1502	614	1463	1082	251	1139	206	1046	167
1012	172	628	1581	1120	237	580	1473	1060	285	693	1533
1086	1483	1135	210	678	163	654	187	703	1506	1110	1459
1019	1550	626	1583	611	230	587	254	1058	287	1043	1526
657	1540	1137	208	621	1456	1089	244	705	1504	1053	160
1015	174	630	1579	1123	234	583	1470	1062	283	691	1530
638	1487	1031	218	674	1571	1070	191	599	1514	1106	275
1144	261	664	1449	1036	201	712	1557	1096	153	604	1497
642	247	1027	222	1050	1567	1074	1543	595	1518	618	271
719	170	662	1451	1127	1490	1151	1466	1094	155	695	194
645	1485	1029	220	681	1564	1077	184	597	1516	1108	268
1147	258	1098	151	1039	198	715	1554	666	1447	607	1494

D = 5

FIGURE 11–3 continued

1649	764	1604	797	1685	848	65	908	20	941	101	992
135	975	1671	730	27	922	1719	838	87	874	1618	778
61	972	24	937	37	996	1645	828	1608	793	1621	852
140	893	1673	728	116	917	1724	749	89	872	1700	773
1654	759	22	939	1690	843	70	903	1606	795	106	987
144	973	1669	732	36	913	1728	829	85	876	1620	769
1661	824	128	929	1625	740	77	968	1712	785	41	884
3	898	1635	862	111	958	1587	754	51	1006	1695	814
1657	768	132	925	1681	744	73	912	1716	781	97	888
1592	833	1637	860	1616	809	8	977	53	1004	32	953
1666	826	130	927	1630	735	82	963	1714	783	39	879
12	889	49	1008	120	949	1596	745	1633	864	1704	805

D = 6

1379	530	419	1214	1343	446	371	1250	1427	494	335	1166
297	1180	1353	568	405	1240	1305	460	345	1288	1413	520
1363	474	307	1230	1399	558	355	1194	1315	510	391	1278
422	1271	1382	443	314	1211	1430	551	374	1163	1322	491
1372	537	412	1221	1336	453	364	1257	1420	501	328	1173
294	1183	1350	570	402	1243	1302	463	343	1291	1410	523
1367	470	302	1226	1403	554	359	1190	1319	515	395	1274
429	1264	1389	436	321	1204	1437	544	381	1156	1329	484
1375	534	415	1219	1339	450	367	1254	1422	498	331	1170
290	1187	1355	575	398	1247	1298	467	338	1286	1406	527
1360	477	304	1233	1396	561	352	1197	1312	513	388	1281
426	1267	1386	439	318	1207	1434	547	378	1159	1326	487

D = 7

FIGURE 11-3 continued

1073	185	1028	221	1112	272	641	1481	596	1517	680	1568
718	1558	1102	147	610	1491	1150	255	670	1443	1035	195
649	241	708	1501	1056	1464	1081	1537	1140	205	624	168
584	176	1061	284	1121	1529	1016	1472	629	1580	689	233
1071	190	591	1522	1107	274	639	1486	1023	226	675	1570
720	1560	1093	156	601	1489	1152	264	661	1452	1033	193
1085	245	704	1505	1052	164	653	1541	1136	209	620	1460
586	1467	1066	279	694	1527	1018	171	634	1575	1126	231
1069	1477	600	1513	684	276	637	181	1032	217	1116	1572
1148	1556	1097	152	605	197	716	260	665	1448	1037	1493
1083	243	699	1510	1047	166	651	1546	1131	214	622	1462
588	1476	625	1584	685	1525	1020	180	1057	288	1117	229

D = 8

71	971	14	947	38	986	1655	827	1598	803	1622	842
1588	748	88	1005	1696	777	136	897	1636	729	117	957
1651	763	1602	799	1686	846	67	907	18	943	102	990
1718	830	95	866	1619	779	134	974	1679	722	35	923
81	964	1605	784	45	988	1653	820	129	940	1629	736
1722	750	91	870	1699	775	138	894	1675	726	115	919
83	911	1706	791	98	878	1667	767	122	935	1682	734
1720	837	52	873	1612	813	4	981	1672	861	28	921
79	967	1710	787	42	882	1663	823	126	931	1626	738
2	890	59	998	119	959	1586	746	1643	854	1703	815
69	909	1713	796	105	880	1665	760	21	928	1684	844
1590	834	1639	858	1615	811	6	978	55	1002	31	955

D = 9

FIGURE 11–3 continued

353	1196	1313	512	389	1280	1361	476	305	1232	1397	560
1431	550	375	1162	1323	490	423	1270	1383	442	315	1210
361	1260	1417	504	325	1176	1369	540	409	1224	1333	456
1304	461	344	1289	1412	521	296	1181	1352	569	404	1241
358	1191	1318	507	394	1275	1366	471	310	1227	1402	555
1440	541	384	1164	1332	481	432	1261	1381	433	324	1201
365	1256	1424	500	329	1172	1373	536	413	1217	1337	452
1299	466	339	1294	1407	526	291	1186	1347	574	399	1246
349	1200	1309	505	385	1284	1357	480	312	1236	1393	564
1436	545	377	1157	1328	485	428	1265	1388	440	320	1205
370	1251	1426	495	334	1167	1378	531	418	1215	1342	447
1308	457	348	1285	1416	517	300	1177	1356	565	408	1237

$$D = 10$$

659	1538	698	1511	623	1454	1091	242	1130	215	1055	158
1017	177	633	1576	1125	232	585	1468	1065	280	688	1528
1075	1482	1026	223	679	270	643	186	594	1519	1111	1566
1142	263	671	1442	1034	203	710	1559	1103	146	602	1499
652	1545	1132	213	616	1461	1084	249	700	1509	1048	165
1014	175	631	1578	1122	235	582	1471	1063	282	690	1531
647	1478	1022	227	683	1562	1079	182	590	1523	1115	266
1149	256	669	1444	1041	196	717	1552	1101	148	609	1492
655	1542	1134	211	619	1458	1087	246	702	1507	1051	162
578	179	635	1574	1118	1535	1010	1475	1067	278	686	239
640	1480	1024	225	676	1569	1072	189	592	1521	1113	273
1146	259	1099	150	1038	199	714	1555	667	1446	606	1495

$$D = 11$$

FIGURE 11–3. ORTHOGONAL SECTIONS PARALLEL TO THE FRONT

659	1538	698	1511	623	1454	1091	242	1130	215	1055	158
353	1196	1313	512	389	1280	1361	476	305	1232	1397	560
71	971	14	947	38	986	1655	827	1598	803	1622	842
1073	185	1028	221	1112	272	641	1481	596	1517	680	1568
1379	530	419	1214	1343	446	371	1250	1427	494	335	1166
1649	764	1604	797	1685	848	65	908	20	941	101	992
650	1547	707	1502	614	1463	1082	251	1139	206	1046	167
356	1193	1316	509	392	1277	1364	473	308	1229	1400	557
74	962	131	926	47	887	1658	818	1715	782	1631	743
1088	188	1133	212	1109	161	656	1484	701	1508	677	1457
1370	539	410	1223	1334	455	362	1259	1418	503	326	1175
1652	761	1601	800	1688	845	68	905	17	944	104	989

R = 11

FIGURE 11–4. TOP ORTHOGONAL SECTION

659	353	71	1073	1379	1649	650	356	74	1088	1370	1652
1017	1431	1588	718	297	135	1012	1438	1593	711	292	142
1075	361	1651	649	1363	61	1086	372	1650	660	1362	84
1142	1304	1718	584	422	140	1019	1301	1727	581	431	5
652	358	81	1071	1372	1654	657	351	76	1078	1377	1647
1014	1440	1722	720	294	144	1015	1429	1591	577	295	133
647	365	83	1085	1367	1661	638	368	62	1076	1358	1664
1149	1299	1720	586	429	3	1144	1306	1725	579	424	10
655	349	79	1069	1375	1657	642	360	78	1080	1374	1656
578	1436	2	1148	290	1592	719	1433	11	1145	299	1721
640	370	69	1083	1360	1666	645	363	64	1090	1365	1659
1146	1308	1590	588	426	12	1147	1297	1723	709	427	1

C = 0

FIGURE 11–5. LEFT SIDE ORTHOGONAL SECTION

659	1538	698	1511	623	1454	1091	242	1130	215	1055	158
1431	550	375	1162	1323	490	423	1270	1383	442	315	1210
1651	763	1602	799	1686	846	67	907	18	943	102	990
584	176	1061	284	1121	1529	1016	1472	629	1580	689	233
1372	537	412	1221	1336	453	364	1257	1420	501	328	1173
144	973	1669	752	36	913	1728	829	85	876	1620	769
638	1487	1031	218	674	1571	1070	191	599	1514	1106	275
1306	459	346	1287	1414	519	298	1179	1354	567	406	1239
78	966	1711	786	43	883	1662	822	127	930	1627	739
1145	1553	1100	149	608	200	713	257	668	1445	1040	1496
1365	472	309	1228	1401	556	357	1192	1317	508	393	1276
1	900	60	997	109	960	1585	756	1644	853	1693	816

FIGURE 11–6. DIAGONAL SECTION PERPENDICULAR TO THE LEFT-HAND SIDE SHOWING TWO OF THE SPACE DIAGONALS

1652	761	1601	800	1688	845	68	905	17	944	104	989
292	1185	1348	573	400	1245	1300	465	340	1293	1408	525
660	252	697	1512	1045	1453	1092	1548	1129	216	613	157
1727	839	86	875	1610	770	143	983	1670	731	26	914
351	1198	1311	514	387	1282	1359	478	303	1234	1395	562
1015	174	630	1579	1123	234	583	1470	1062	283	691	1530
1661	824	128	929	1625	740	77	968	1712	785	41	884
429	1264	1389	436	321	1204	1437	544	381	1156	1329	484
1069	1477	600	1513	684	276	637	181	1032	217	1116	1572
2	890	59	998	119	959	1586	746	1643	854	1703	815
370	1251	1426	495	334	1167	1378	531	418	1215	1342	447
1146	259	1099	150	1038	199	714	1555	667	1446	606	1495

FIGURE 11–7. DIAGONAL SECTIONS PERPENDICULAR TO THE LEFT-HAND SIDE SHOWING THE OTHER TWO SPACE DIAGONALS

How about perfect magic cubes of this order? In Chapter 3 we proved that a fourth-order perfect magic cube could not exist. Using the generating characteristics of Case 4 and the calculators at the Dickinson College Computation Center, we constructed a $20 \times 20 \times 20$ perfect magic cube that has been thoroughly checked and found to be correct. The front orthogonal section of this cube is shown in Figure 11–2. The magic constant is 80,010. Although we have not attempted to construct any larger magic cubes of this type because of the difficulties resulting from size, we believe that the method employed (which involved making transfers of the type described in the last chapter) is applicable to any doubly-even-order cube of higher order.

The case of the $12 \times 12 \times 12$ cube was the only one in doubt, but we are proud to be able to show what we believe to be the first $12 \times 12 \times 12$ perfect magic cube ever constructed (see Figures 11–3 through 11–7). It is a difficult cube to construct and required the development of several new basic principles before it could be completed.

The first breakthrough (which did not actually involve a new principle) was the discovery of the generating characteristics shown below as Case 10:

$$\begin{vmatrix} 6 & 2 & 3 \\ 2 & 3 & 6 \\ 3 & 6 & 2 \end{vmatrix}_N \qquad \Delta = 1 \bmod 12$$

The controlling characteristics for the orthogonals are shown in Figure 11–8. (It is coincidental that these characteristics are the same as the generating characteristics for Case 10.) The controlling characteristics of the main diagonals are 1, 3, 4, 5, 8, and 9; for the space diagonals they are 1, 5, 7, and 11.

	x	X	x
Perpendicular to the side	6	2	3
Perpendicular to the top	2	3	6
Perpendicular to the front	3	6	2

FIGURE 11–8. CONTROLLING CHARACTERISTICS OF THE ORTHOGONALS

The next step is to use our standard procedure and the generating characteristics of Case 10 to construct the normal intermediate letter cube. As expected, in the orthogonals (and the space diagonals) of this cube, either the twelve letters appeared once and only once, or six letters appeared two times each, or four letters appeared three times each, or two letters appeared six times each. It is simple to assign the numbers 0 to $(N-1)$ to the letters so as to meet these requirements. Generating a cube with all of the orthogonals and space diagonals correct is very important.

It is with the main diagonals, where we find some of the letters appearing in groups of three (each repeated four times) that we meet our first obstacle. It is not possible to meet the following requirements using the tools so far at our disposal:

$$A + G = B + H = C + I = D + J = E + K = F + L = 12(12-1)/12 = 11$$

and

$$4(A + E + I) + 2w = 4(G + K + C) - 2w = 12(12-1)/2 = 66,$$

where

$$(G - A) \quad \text{or} \quad (C - I) \quad \text{or} \quad (K - E) = w.$$

We were completely stopped until we realized that the same purpose could be accomplished by using

$$A + G = B + H = C + I = D + J = E + K = F + L = 11$$

and

$$4(A + E + I) + u + v = 4(G + K + C) - u - v,$$

where

$$(G - A) \quad \text{or} \quad (C - I) \quad \text{or} \quad (K - E) = u$$

and

$$(G - A) \quad \text{or} \quad (C - I) \quad \text{or} \quad (K - E) = v$$

and

$$4(B + F + J) + x + y = 4(D + H + L) - x - y,$$

where

$$(H - B) \quad \text{or} \quad (L - F) \quad \text{or} \quad (D - J) = x$$

and

$$(H - B) \quad \text{or} \quad (L - F) \quad \text{or} \quad (D - J) = y.$$

We let A = 0, B = 1, C = 2, D = 6, E = 4, F = 8, G = 11, H = 10, I = 9, J = 5, K = 7, and L = 3, which meets the necessary requirements and permits us to make the interchanges necessary to correct the main diagonals in those instances where three letters appeared four times each.

Our next obstacle arose when we found that we could not make all of the required interchanges without violating the requirement that you must avoid interchanging any number that you have interchanged before. We overcame this difficulty when we realized that the requirement was not correctly worded. It should have been worded thus: You must avoid making any interchange between two numbers unless neither *or both* of the numbers involved in the interchange have been previously subjected to an interchange. It should be obvious that when both of the numbers involved have been interchanged, the two interchanges much be of the same type letter, that is, they must both affect the lowercase (or capital, or italic) letters. Thus we can get around the problem by going back and making a few, otherwise unnecessary, interchanges.

This all sounds very complicated—and it is. It is possible, however, and the result is a 12 × 12 × 12 perfect magic cube, as shown in Figures 11–3 through 11–7. All of the orthogonals, all of the main diagonals of the orthogonal sections, and all of the space diagonals add to the magic constant, 10,374.

Chapter 12

Singly-Even Perfect Magic Cubes

As far as we know, ours is the first discussion anywhere of singly-even perfect magic cubes. We are particularly pleased to show such a cube here, which is, needless to say, a very difficult cube to construct—by far the most difficult in this book.

This cube, like those discussed previously, is based on the basic cyclical principles combined with the use of an intermediate letter cube and the interchange of carefully selected pairs of numbers. That this method made it possible to construct this cube is further proof, if such proof is needed, of its great strength and flexibility.

For orthogonals	1, 2, and 4
For main diagonals	1, 2, 3, 5, and 6
For space diagonals	1, 3, 5, and 7

(Note that $\Delta = 9$ is prime to $N = 14$, as required.)

FIGURE 12–1. CONTROLLING CHARACTERISTICS

We constructed the intermediate cube by using the generating characteristics given in Case 3. Taking the controlling characteristics into account (see Figure 12–1), we find that we obtain the expected result and that the orthogonals and main diagonals consist of either fourteen different letters and are automatically correct, or the seven letters A, C, E, G, I, K, M (or B, D, F, H, J, N), each repeated two times. The letters in the space diagonals

116

consist of either fourteen different letters and are automatically correct, or the two letters B and I, each repeated seven times. Although the correct sum of the letters in any given case is 91 (and cannot be divided into two equal parts), if we let A = 0, B = 6, C = 2, D = 4, E = 10, F = 8, G = 12, H = 1, I = 7, J = 3, K = 5, L = 11, M = 9, and N = 13, we will see that

$$2(A + C + E + G + I + K + M) + 1 = 91, \quad \text{and}$$

$$2(B + D + F + H + J + L + N) - 1 = 91.$$

We also note that

$$H - A = J - C = L - E = N - G = +1, \text{ and that}$$

$$B - I = D - K = F - M = -1, \text{ and that}$$

$$B + I = 13,$$

as required.

It follows that if we are quite careful in making the necessary interchanges (as discussed in Chapter 11), we will be able to correct the orthogonals and main diagonals and, at the same time, not disturb the space diagonals. It is not easy to meet these requirements—up to five interchanges in a given orthogonal or diagonal (three plus one and two minus one interchanges, or two plus one and one minus one interchange, or just one plus one interchange, as the case may be), but it is possible, as we can see in Figure 12–2 (the fourteen orthogonal sections parallel to the front of the cube), Figure 12–3 (the left side orthogonal section), Figure 12–4 (the top orthogonal section), and Figures 12–5 and 12–6 (two diagonal sections, showing the four space diagonals). Remember that in making any interchange between a pair of numbers it is essential that the two numbers differ only in the letter it is desired to correct. For example, you can interchange cBa with cBh when you desire to increase the sum of the numbers in the orthogonals containing the number cBa by 1 and decrease the sum of the numbers in the orthogonals containing the number cBh by 1.

We believe that, the large amount of work involved notwithstanding, the method just described will work for any other larger singly-even cube. It is possible, however, that difficulty may be experienced when 3 or 5 is a factor of N.

1	2392	1912	2137	1082	476	1504	2	2391	1925	2334	1081	475	1503
2327	896	664	1500	207	2597	1718	2132	895	467	1303	208	2584	1717
1509	203	2390	1907	2141	1083	463	1510	22	2389	1908	2142	1084	464
1722	2343	883	670	1296	9	2593	1721	2330	870	669	1309	206	2594
666	1508	3	2394	1910	2130	1089	469	1507	4	2407	1909	2129	1090
2596	1709	2153	875	668	1306	209	2595	1710	2336	890	667	1291	210
1088	465	1512	215	2381	1915	2136	1087	466	1511	6	2382	1916	2135
197	2588	1716	2333	885	672	1308	198	2587	1729	2138	886	671	1307
2131	1078	468	1304	25	2387	1914	2328	1091	663	1499	12	2402	1913
1313	7	2586	1712	2351	887	659	1314	204	2585	1711	2338	888	660
1917	2147	1065	474	1506	205	2383	1918	2134	1080	473	1505	24	2384
470	1312	199	2590	1714	2326	894	665	1311	200	2589	1727	2325	893
2386	1905	2349	1085	472	1502	13	2385	1906	2140	1086	471	1501	14
892	662	1315	19	2577	1720	2332	891	661	1316	202	2578	1719	2331

Back D = 13

560	1559	85	2420	1884	1983	1011	559	1560	86	2419	1883	2180	1026
2612	1689	1977	840	748	1360	291	2611	1690	2160	839	747	1359	292
1028	548	1565	91	2418	1880	1987	1027	743	1566	92	2417	1879	1974
289	2608	1693	2175	827	739	1366	290	2411	1708	2176	828	740	1365
1961	1034	554	1563	88	2618	1882	1976	1033	553	1564	87	2421	1881
1361	294	2610	1682	2167	833	752	1362	293	2413	1681	2182	834	751
1887	2177	1032	536	1567	89	2410	1888	2178	835	549	1568	90	2409
756	1349	282	2616	1702	2179	829	755	1350	281	2615	1687	1984	830
2416	1885	2173	1035	551	1556	95	2415	1886	1964	1036	552	1555	96
832	744	1369	287	2614	1684	2183	817	547	1370	288	2613	1683	2184
94	2412	1889	1979	1023	558	1562	93	2607	1890	1966	1024	557	1561
2171	837	736	1367	284	2422	1685	2172	838	749	1368	283	2617	1686
1557	98	2414	1878	1971	1029	556	1558	97	2609	1877	1986	1030	555
1691	1981	836	746	1371	285	2606	1692	1982	1031	745	1358	286	2605

D = 12

FIGURE 12–2 CONTINUED

2068	1054	531	1377	29	2714	1940	2067	1039	532	1378	30	2517	1939
1191	236	2696	1745	2257	867	720	1178	235	2695	1746	2258	868	523
1935	2072	1056	520	1383	35	2712	1936	2071	1055	519	1384	36	2501
711	1379	38	2705	1749	2246	856	530	1198	233	2706	1750	2259	855
2506	1951	2059	1062	526	1381	31	2505	1938	2060	1061	525	1382	228
862	723	1193	238	2694	1738	2251	861	724	1194	237	2693	1737	2070
34	2494	1944	2065	1060	522	1385	33	2493	1943	2066	1059	717	1400
2264	844	727	1182	240	2518	1744	2263	843	728	1181	239	2699	1743
1387	40	2500	1941	2061	1063	524	1374	39	2499	1942	2062	1064	719
1739	2267	860	716	1187	231	2516	1740	2268	859	715	1188	232	2697
529	1183	234	2495	1945	2063	1051	726	1394	37	2496	1946	2064	1052
2701	1755	2255	866	722	1185	227	2702	1742	2256	865	721	1186	32
1058	527	1375	42	2498	1934	2069	1057	528	1376	55	2497	1933	2266
230	2690	1747	2261	864	718	1189	243	2703	1748	2248	863	521	1190

$$D = 11$$

2475	1785	2012	1124	587	1461	58	2490	1786	1997	1123	784	1476	57
937	565	1457	68	2682	1591	2201	1148	580	1262	263	2667	1592	2202
64	2473	1782	2016	1126	772	1467	63	2474	1781	2015	1139	575	1468
2204	940	781	1267	262	2664	1595	2189	939	782	1268	65	2663	1596
1466	60	2673	1587	2003	1145	582	1465	59	2674	1784	2004	1132	581
1584	2014	932	779	1264	266	2665	1583	2013	1141	780	1263	265	2666
577	1483	61	2466	1775	2010	1144	578	1470	62	2661	1776	2009	1143
2671	1575	2208	941	783	1265	254	2672	1576	2207	942	588	1280	253
1147	761	1261	264	2486	1773	2005	952	776	1458	67	2471	1788	2006
260	2669	1586	2212	944	576	1271	259	2670	1585	2211	943	757	1272
2008	1136	585	1463	66	2468	1791	1993	1135	586	1464	261	2467	1792
1270	256	2477	1783	2199	949	778	1269	255	2478	1588	2200	950	763
1779	2210	1128	583	1459	70	2470	1780	2209	945	584	1460	69	2469
773	1288	272	2662	1579	2205	934	774	1273	257	2465	1594	2192	947

$$D = 10$$

FIGURE 12–2 CONTINUED

1406	142	2545	1855	2236	1110	419	1405	141	2546	1870	2039	1095	406
1676	2229	923	593	1205	348	2528	1675	2230	924	594	1206	347	2737
407	1411	148	2529	1865	2043	1112	394	1412	147	2726	1866	2044	1111
2719	1876	2036	912	599	1225	346	2734	1665	2035	911	600	1212	345
1117	399	1410	354	2533	1867	2032	1118	400	1409	143	2534	1868	2031
349	2721	1667	2238	918	611	1207	154	2722	1668	2237	917	598	1208
2234	1116	395	1218	146	2522	1873	2233	1115	396	1413	145	2535	1874
1210	352	2727	1673	2040	899	615	1209	351	2728	1674	2235	900	602
1858	2033	1120	397	1416	152	2724	1871	2034	1119	398	1415	151	2527
603	1216	344	2725	1669	2240	916	590	1215	343	2530	1670	2239	915
2524	1680	2232	1108	403	1407	150	2523	1875	2231	1107	404	1422	149
921	596	1214	158	2729	1672	2227	922	595	1213	339	2730	1671	2228
153	2525	1863	2041	1114	401	1403	350	2540	1864	2042	1113	402	1404
2038	919	591	1414	342	2718	1663	2037	920	592	1231	341	2731	1678

D = 9

1165	686	1434	113	2364	1813	2124	1166	489	1447	114	2363	1814	2123
320	2569	1619	2314	979	677	1233	123	2570	1620	2299	980	678	1234
2127	1154	673	1454	134	2375	1613	2128	1153	674	1439	119	2376	1796
1240	317	2565	1610	2316	968	487	1239	318	2566	1623	2315	967	684
1811	2115	1173	483	1438	116	2365	1812	2312	1174	484	1437	115	2380
682	1236	321	2357	1611	2322	974	681	1235	322	2568	1612	2321	973
2367	1818	2318	1171	479	1442	118	2368	1621	2303	1172	676	1245	117
969	490	1238	324	2559	1603	2320	970	685	1237	323	2574	1604	2319
124	2373	1816	2118	1175	481	1430	319	2374	1815	2103	1176	482	1429
2309	971	477	1244	316	2571	1809	2310	972	478	1243	329	2572	1614
1436	121	2370	1820	2120	1164	683	1435	122	2369	1819	2105	1163	488
1616	2311	963	679	1242	311	2575	1615	2116	978	680	1241	312	2576
486	1432	126	2553	1807	2126	1170	485	1431	125	2372	1808	2125	1169
2563	1622	2122	975	675	1246	314	2564	1817	2107	976	480	1441	313

D = 8

FIGURE 12–2   CONTINUED

1842	2095	983	630	1518	170	2461	1841	2096	998	433	1517	169	2462
622	1332	376	2653	1648	2286	797	621	1317	375	2458	1647	2285	798
2460	1837	2099	985	617	1538	176	2459	1838	2100	790	618	1523	175
785	432	1324	373	2650	1651	2288	786	627	1323	388	2649	1652	2287
171	2660	1840	2088	991	427	1536	172	2449	1825	2087	1006	428	1535
2293	791	626	1516	391	2455	1640	2294	792	625	1319	378	2456	1639
1525	173	2451	1845	2094	989	423	1526	384	2452	1846	2093	990	424
1646	2291	787	434	1322	366	2657	1645	2292	802	629	1321	365	2658
426	1514	193	2457	1844	2090	993	425	1513	180	2654	1843	2089	994
2656	1642	2295	789	421	1328	372	2655	1641	2296	986	422	1341	371
981	628	1520	191	2439	1847	2092	982	445	1519	178	2454	1848	2091
382	2464	1644	2284	795	624	1326	381	2645	1643	2283	796	623	1325
2097	987	430	1320	195	2651	1835	2098	988	429	1515	182	2652	1836
1329	369	2647	1650	2290	793	619	1330	188	2648	1649	2289	794	620

D = 7

15	2405	1926	2151	1067	462	1490	16	2406	1911	2348	1068	461	1489
2145	882	650	1289	221	2583	1732	2342	881	649	1290	222	2598	1731
1495	21	2404	1922	2155	1069	449	1496	8	2403	1921	2156	1070	646
1736	2329	869	460	1310	219	2579	1735	2344	884	459	1491	220	2580
456	1494	18	2408	1924	2144	1075	651	1493	17	2393	1923	2143	1076
2582	1724	2335	889	654	1292	27	2581	1723	2350	876	653	1305	224
1074	452	1497	201	2395	1929	2150	1073	451	1498	20	2396	1930	2149
211	2601	1730	2347	871	658	1294	212	2602	1715	2152	872	657	1293
2341	1092	453	1486	11	2401	1928	2146	1077	454	1485	26	2388	1927
1299	217	2600	1726	2337	873	645	1300	218	2599	1725	2352	874	450
1931	2133	1079	656	1492	23	2397	1932	2148	1066	655	1295	10	2398
652	1298	214	2604	1728	2340	880	455	1297	213	2603	1713	2339	879
2400	1920	2139	1071	458	1488	223	2399	1919	2154	1072	457	1487	28
878	647	1301	5	2592	1734	2346	877	648	1302	216	2591	1733	2345

D = 6

FIGURE 12–2 CONTINUED

545	1545	100	2434	1897	1969	1025	546	1546	295	2433	1898	1970	1012
2626	1703	1963	826	734	1346	306	2625	1704	2174	825	733	1345	305
1014	534	1551	301	2432	1894	1973	1013	533	1552	106	2431	1893	1988
108	2426	1903	2161	813	753	1352	303	2621	1694	2162	814	754	1351
1975	1020	540	1549	297	2436	1896	1962	1019	539	1550	298	2435	1699
1347	308	2624	1696	2181	819	738	1348	307	2427	1695	2168	820	737
1901	1967	1017	550	1554	299	2423	1902	1968	1018	535	1553	104	2424
741	1363	296	2630	1688	2165	815	742	1364	99	2629	1701	2166	816
2430	1899	2159	1022	538	1542	109	2429	1900	1978	1021	537	1541	110
818	730	1355	105	2628	1698	2169	831	729	1356	302	2627	1697	2170
304	2622	1707	1965	1010	544	1548	107	2425	1904	1980	1009	543	1547
2157	823	750	1353	101	2632	1700	2158	824	735	1354	102	2631	1895
1544	112	2428	1892	1985	1015	542	1543	111	2623	1891	1972	1016	541
1705	2163	822	731	1357	103	2619	1706	2164	821	732	1372	300	2620

D = 5

2250	1040	517	1195	43	2504	1954	2249	1053	518	1392	44	2503	1953
1177	250	2710	1759	2047	854	706	1192	249	2709	1760	2244	853	705
1949	2057	1042	506	1397	49	2698	1950	2058	1041	505	1398	50	2515
725	1197	248	2692	1763	2260	841	712	1184	247	2691	1764	2049	842
2519	1937	2045	1047	512	1396	45	2520	1952	2046	1048	511	1395	242
848	709	1179	252	2708	1751	2265	847	710	1180	251	2511	1752	2252
48	2508	1958	2052	1046	507	1399	47	2507	1957	2051	1045	704	1386
2054	858	713	1391	226	2700	1758	2053	857	714	1196	225	2713	1757
1373	54	2514	1955	2243	1050	510	1388	53	2513	1956	2048	1049	509
1754	2254	846	702	1201	245	2502	1753	2253	845	701	1202	246	2711
515	1393	52	2510	1959	2050	1038	516	1380	51	2509	1960	2245	1037
2715	1741	2241	851	708	1199	241	2716	1756	2242	852	707	1200	46
1044	513	1389	56	2512	1947	2055	1043	514	1390	41	2707	1948	2056
244	2704	1761	2247	850	703	1203	229	2689	1762	2262	849	508	1204

D = 4

FIGURE 12–2   CONTINUED

2489	1772	2194	1138	573	1475	71	2476	1771	2011	1137	574	1462	72
951	775	1275	278	2668	1577	2187	938	762	1276	277	2485	1578	2188
78	2487	1767	2002	1140	562	1482	273	2488	1768	2001	1125	561	1481
2190	925	768	1281	276	2678	1581	2203	926	767	1282	79	2677	1582
1480	73	2491	1769	1989	1131	764	1479	74	2492	1770	1990	1146	567
1569	2196	946	765	1277	280	2680	1570	2195	931	570	1278	279	2679
564	1469	76	2480	1789	1996	1130	563	1484	271	2479	1790	1995	1129
2685	1589	1998	927	769	1279	267	2686	1590	2193	928	770	1266	268
1133	579	1471	82	2472	1787	1991	1134	566	1472	81	2681	1774	1992
274	2684	1571	2198	930	758	1285	77	2683	1572	2197	929	771	1286
1994	1122	571	1477	80	2481	1777	2007	1121	572	1478	275	2482	1778
1283	270	2687	1573	2185	936	568	1284	269	2688	1574	2186	935	777
1765	2000	1142	569	1474	84	2484	1766	1999	1127	766	1473	83	2483
760	1274	258	2676	1593	2191	948	759	1287	75	2675	1580	2206	933

$$D = 3$$

1420	155	2531	1869	2026	1096	601	1419	156	2532	1660	2025	1109	616
1662	2216	909	607	1219	166	2738	1857	2215	910	608	1220	165	2723
393	1426	162	2543	1851	2030	1098	408	1425	161	2740	1852	2029	1097
2733	1666	2218	898	613	1211	360	2720	1679	2217	897	614	1226	163
1104	413	1424	340	2547	1853	2017	1103	414	1423	157	2548	1854	2018
167	2735	1653	2223	904	597	1221	364	2736	1654	2224	903	612	1222
2024	1102	409	1428	356	2536	1859	2023	1101	410	1427	159	2521	1860
1224	338	2741	1659	2222	914	405	1223	337	2742	1856	2221	913	420
1872	2020	1106	411	1402	362	2542	1661	2019	1105	412	1401	361	2541
589	1230	358	2739	1655	2225	902	604	1229	357	2544	1656	2226	901
2537	1861	2022	1094	417	1421	164	2538	1862	2021	1093	418	1408	359
907	609	1228	144	2743	1657	2213	908	610	1227	353	2744	1658	2214
363	2539	1849	2028	1100	415	1418	168	2526	1850	2027	1099	416	1417
2220	905	605	1232	160	2732	1677	2219	906	606	1217	355	2717	1664

$$D = 2$$

FIGURE 12–2   CONTINUED

1151	504	1448	128	2377	1799	2110	1152	699	1433	127	2378	1800	2109
333	2555	1606	2300	966	691	1247	138	2556	1605	2313	965	692	1248
2114	1168	491	1440	120	2361	1795	2113	1167	492	1453	133	2558	1810
1254	331	2551	1624	2106	954	697	1253	332	2552	1609	2301	953	698
1798	2101	1159	497	1452	130	2379	1797	2102	1160	694	1451	129	2366
696	1250	336	2371	1597	2308	960	695	1249	335	2554	1598	2307	959
2353	1804	2108	1157	493	1456	328	2354	1607	2121	1158	494	1455	327
955	700	1251	310	2573	1617	2306	956	503	1252	309	2560	1618	2305
137	2359	1802	2104	1161	495	1443	334	2360	1801	2117	1162	496	1444
2323	957	687	1257	330	2557	1600	2324	958	688	1258	315	2362	1599
1450	135	2356	1806	2302	1150	501	1449	136	2355	1805	2119	1149	502
1602	2297	977	693	1256	325	2561	1601	2298	964	498	1255	326	2562
500	1446	139	2567	1793	2112	1156	499	1445	140	2358	1794	2111	1155
2549	1608	2304	961	689	1260	132	2550	1803	2317	962	690	1259	131

$$D = 1$$

1828	2081	997	644	1532	183	2447	1827	2082	984	447	1531	184	2448
636	1318	390	2443	1634	2272	811	635	1331	389	2640	1633	2271	812
2642	1824	2085	999	436	1524	190	2445	1823	2086	1000	435	1537	189
799	446	1338	387	2635	1638	2274	800	641	1337	374	2636	1637	2273
185	2450	1826	2074	1005	441	1522	186	2463	1839	2073	992	638	1521
2279	805	640	1334	181	2637	1626	2280	806	639	1333	392	2638	1625
1539	187	2437	1831	2080	1003	437	1540	370	2438	1832	2079	1004	438
1632	2277	801	448	1335	380	2643	1631	2278	788	643	1336	379	2644
440	1528	179	2639	1830	2076	1007	439	1527	194	2444	1829	2075	1008
2446	1627	2281	803	632	1342	386	2641	1628	2282	804	631	1327	385
995	642	1533	177	2453	1834	2078	996	431	1534	192	2440	1833	2077
368	2646	1630	2270	809	637	1340	367	2659	1629	2269	810	442	1339
2083	1001	444	1530	377	2441	1821	2084	1002	443	1529	196	2442	1822
1343	383	2634	1636	2276	807	633	1344	174	2633	1635	2275	808	634

Front $D = 0$

FIGURE 12–2. FOURTEEN ORTHOGONAL SECTIONS PARALLEL TO THE
FRONT

1	560	2068	2475	1406	1165	1842	15	545	2250	2489	1420	1151	1828
2327	2612	1191	937	1676	320	622	2145	2626	1177	951	1662	333	636
1509	1028	1935	64	407	2127	2460	1495	1014	1949	78	393	2114	2642
1722	289	711	2204	2719	1240	785	1736	108	725	2190	2733	1254	799
666	1961	2506	1466	1117	1811	171	456	1975	2519	1480	1104	1798	185
2596	1361	862	1584	349	682	2293	2582	1347	848	1569	167	696	2279
1088	1887	34	577	2234	2367	1525	1074	1901	48	564	2024	2353	1539
197	756	2264	2671	1210	969	1646	211	741	2054	2685	1224	955	1632
2131	2416	1387	1147	1858	124	426	2341	2430	1373	1133	1872	137	440
1313	832	1739	260	603	2309	2656	1299	818	1754	274	589	2323	2446
1917	94	529	2008	2524	1436	981	1931	304	515	1994	2537	1450	995
470	2171	2701	1270	921	1616	382	652	2157	2715	1283	907	1602	368
2386	1557	1058	1779	153	486	2097	2400	1544	1044	1765	363	500	2083
892	1691	230	773	2038	2563	1329	878	1705	244	760	2220	2549	1343

C = 0

FIGURE 12–3. LEFT SIDE ORTHOGONAL SECTION

1	2392	1912	2137	1082	476	1504	2	2391	1925	2334	1081	475	1503
560	1559	85	2420	1884	1983	1011	559	1560	86	2419	1883	2180	1026
2068	1054	531	1377	29	2714	1940	2067	1039	532	1378	30	2517	1939
2475	1785	2012	1124	587	1461	58	2490	1786	1997	1123	784	1476	57
1406	142	2545	1855	2236	1110	419	1405	141	2546	1870	2039	1095	406
1165	686	1434	113	2364	1813	2124	1166	489	1447	114	2363	1814	2123
1842	2095	983	630	1518	170	2461	1841	2096	998	433	1517	169	2462
15	2405	1926	2151	1067	462	1490	16	2406	1911	2348	1068	461	1489
545	1545	100	2434	1897	1969	1025	546	1546	295	2433	1898	1970	1012
2250	1040	517	1195	43	2504	1954	2249	1053	518	1392	44	2503	1953
2489	1772	2194	1138	573	1475	71	2476	1771	2011	1137	574	1462	72
1420	155	2531	1869	2026	1096	601	1419	156	2532	1660	2025	1109	616
1151	504	1448	128	2377	1799	2110	1152	699	1433	127	2378	1800	2109
1828	2081	997	644	1532	183	2447	1827	2082	984	447	1531	184	2448

R = 13

FIGURE 12–4. TOP ORTHOGONAL SECTION

1	2392	1912	2137	1082	476	1504	2	2391	1925	2334	1081	475	1503
2612	1689	1977	840	748	1360	291	2611	1690	2160	839	747	1359	292
1935	2072	1056	520	1383	35	2712	1936	2071	1055	519	1384	36	2501
2204	940	781	1267	262	2664	1595	2189	939	782	1268	65	2663	1596
1117	399	1410	354	2533	1867	2032	1118	400	1409	143	2534	1868	2031
682	1236	321	2357	1611	2322	974	681	1235	322	2568	1612	2321	973
1525	173	2451	1845	2094	989	423	1526	384	2452	1846	2093	990	424
211	2601	1730	2347	871	658	1294	212	2602	1715	2152	872	657	1293
2430	1899	2159	1022	538	1542	109	2429	1900	1978	1021	537	1541	110
1754	2254	846	702	1201	245	2502	1753	2253	845	701	1202	246	2711
1994	1122	571	1477	80	2481	1777	2007	1211	572	1478	275	2482	1778
907	609	1228	144	2743	1657	2213	908	610	1227	353	2744	1658	2214
500	1446	139	2567	1793	2112	1156	499	1445	140	2358	1794	2111	1155
1343	383	2634	1636	2276	807	633	1344	174	2633	1635	2275	808	634

FIGURE 12–5. DIAGONAL SECTION PERPENDICULAR TO LEFT-HAND SIDE
SHOWING TWO OF THE SPACE DIAGONALS

1828	2081	997	644	1532	183	2447	1827	2082	984	447	1531	184	2448
333	2555	1606	2300	966	691	1247	138	2556	1605	2313	965	692	1248
393	1426	162	2543	1851	2030	1098	408	1425	161	2740	1852	2029	1097
2190	925	768	1281	276	2678	1581	2203	926	767	1282	79	2677	1582
2519	1937	2045	1047	512	1396	45	2520	1952	2046	1048	511	1395	242
1347	308	2624	1696	2181	819	738	1348	307	2427	1695	2168	820	737
1074	452	1497	201	2395	1929	2150	1073	451	1498	20	2396	1930	2149
1646	2291	787	434	1322	366	2657	1645	2292	802	629	1321	365	2658
124	2373	1816	2118	1175	481	1430	319	2374	1815	2103	1176	482	1429
603	1216	344	2725	1669	2240	916	590	1215	343	2530	1670	2239	915
2008	1136	585	1463	66	2468	1791	1993	1135	586	1464	261	2467	1792
2701	1755	2255	866	722	1185	227	2702	1742	2256	865	721	1186	32
1557	98	2414	1878	1971	1029	556	1558	97	2609	1877	1986	1030	555
892	662	1315	19	2577	1720	2332	891	661	1316	202	2578	1719	2331

FIGURE 12–6. DIAGONAL SECTION PERPENDICULAR TO THE LEFT-HAND
SIDE SHOWING THE OTHER TWO SPACE DIAGONALS

Part II

Mathematical Proofs

Chapter 13

Extension of the New Cyclical Method to Three Dimensions

The derivation of the requirements to construct a magic cube of order N by an extension of our New Cyclical Method is straightforward.[1] We shall operate with the numbers 0 to $(N^3 - 1)$ rather than the numbers 1 to N^3. As in the two-dimension case, this involves no loss in generality since we can always convert our modified cube into a standard one by adding the number 1 to the number in each cell. We will express all numbers to the base N, that is, we shall express any given number as $xN^2 + XN + x$, where x, X, and x take on all possible values from 0 to $(N-1)$.

Remember that we are dealing with cyclical steps and that cell [i,j,k] and cell [i+uN, j+vN, k+wN] (where u, v, and w equal 0 or any integer, plus or minus) are equivalent. As in the two-dimension case where we needed the regular two-dimension step (C, R) and the two-dimension cross-step (C+c, R+r), we will need a regular three-dimension step (C, R, D) in going from any number $xN^2 + XN + x$ to $xN^2 + XN + (x+1)$ (x is any number from 0 to $(N-2)$), a three-dimension cross-step (C+c, R+r, D+d) in going from $xN^2 + XN + x$ to $xN^2 + (X+1)N + 0$ (when x equals $(N-1)$), and a second three-dimension cross-step

---

1. For the New Cyclical Method see William H. Benson and Oswald Jacoby, *New Recreations with Magic Squares* (New York: Dover Publications, 1976), pp. 43–69, 163–171. A selection from pages 43–47 is reprinted in the Appendix.

$(C+c+c, R+r+r, D+d+d)$ in going from xN^2+XN+x to $(x+1)N^2+(0)N+0$ (when both X and x equal $(N-1)$).

If we start with the number aAa (or 000) in cell [0, 0, 0] and follow a normal three-dimension extension of the method employed in generating a two-dimension magic square, the number xN^2+XN+x will fall in cell [c', r', d'] (the cell c' columns to the right, r' rows up, and d' cells back), where

$$c' \equiv cx + cX + Cx \mod N$$

$$r' \equiv rx + rX + Rx \mod N$$

$$d' \equiv dx + dX + Dx \mod N$$

From the basic theory of linear equations we know that for these equations to be consistent and for the values of x, X, and x to be unique—that is, for any given set of values of c', r', and d', there will be one, and only one, set of values of x, X, and x that will make the three equations correct—the necessary and sufficient condition is that the determinant formed by the coefficients of x, X, and x be prime to N. In other words, if the determinant

$$\Delta = \begin{vmatrix} c & c & C \\ r & r & R \\ d & d & D \end{vmatrix} = - \begin{vmatrix} C & R & D \\ c & r & d \\ c & r & d \end{vmatrix}$$

is·prime to N, then every number will fall into a separate cell; and if it is not prime to N, there will be duplication and some of the cells will contain more than one number (and some will be empty). From the same theory we also know that when Δ is prime to N, the solution to these three equations is

$$x \equiv (c'(rD-Rd)-r'(cD-Cd)+d'(cR-Cr))/\Delta \mod N$$

$$X \equiv (-c'(rD-Rd)+r'(cD-Cd)-d'(cR-Cr))/\Delta \mod N$$

$$x \equiv (c'(rd-rd)-r'(cd-cd)+d'(cr-cr))/\Delta \mod N$$

Now let us examine in more detail the value of x (the "units" digit) in the orthogonals perpendicular to the left side orthogonal section. In particular, consider the orthogonal composed of the cells $c' = 0, 1, 2, \ldots, (N-1)$, $r' = u$ and $d' = t$ (where u and t are fixed constants). Then

$$x \equiv (0(rd - rd) - u(cd - cd) + t(cr - cr))/\Delta \quad \text{mod } N$$

$$x \equiv (1(rd - rd) - u(cd - cd) + t(cr - cr))/\Delta \quad \text{mod } N$$

$$x \equiv (2(rd - rd) - u(cd - cd) + t(cr - cr))/\Delta \quad \text{mod } N$$

. . . .

$$x \equiv (N-1)(rd - rd) - u(cd - cd) + t(cr - cr))/\Delta \quad \text{mod } N$$

Thus we see that the value of x in cell [0, u, t] will equal

$$[0, u, t] \equiv (-u(cd - cd) + t(cr - cr))/\Delta \quad \text{mod } N$$

and the number in cell [1, u, t] will equal the number in cell [0, u, t] plus $(rd - rd)/\Delta \mod N$; the number in cell [2, u, t] will equal the number in cell [1, u, t] plus the same amount, namely, $(rd - rd)/\Delta \mod N$; and so on, the number in each cell being $(rd - rd)/\Delta \mod N$ greater than the number in the preceding cell.

It follows that if $(rd - rd)/\Delta \mod N$ is prime to N, lowercase letters in the intermediate cube (which represent the "units" digits) will each appear once and only once. An analysis of the effect of the controlling characteristic $(rd - rd)$ shows that the effect of its not being prime to N is just what we would have expected. (Note that here we have dropped "division by Δ" and the term "mod N." In all cases "mod N" is understood and "division by Δ," while necessary to determine the exact difference between adjacent cells, has no effect on the determination of the greatest common divisor of the controlling characteristic and N.) Let us designate the greatest common divisor of $(rd - rd)$ and N as s. Then there will be N/s different lowercase letters, each appearing s times, in the orthogonal in question. A similar analysis can be made of the "tens" digits (capital letters) and the "hundreds" digits (italics) for these orthogonals as well as for those perpendicular to the top and front of the cube. The result of such an analysis is shown in Figure 3–3.

Let us now consider the main diagonals of the orthogonal sections parallel to the left side, selecting, for example, the one where c' equals v. Then the "units" digits of one of the main diagonals becomes

$$x \equiv (v(rd - rd) - 0(cd - cd) + 0(cr - cr))/\Delta \mod N$$

$$x \equiv (v(rd - rd) - 1(cd - cd) + 1(cr - cr))/\Delta \mod N$$

$$x \equiv (v(rd - rd) - 2(cd - cd) + 2(cr - cr))/\Delta \mod N$$

$$. \quad . \quad . \quad . \quad . \quad . \quad . \quad . \quad . \quad . \quad . \quad . \quad . \quad . \quad .$$

$$x \equiv (v(rd - rd) - (N - 1)(cd - cd) + (N - 1)(cr - cr))/\Delta \mod N$$

Here each number in the sequence is

$$(-(cd - cd) + (cr - cr))/\Delta \mod N$$

greater than the preceding one. It follows that for this particular diagonal the controlling characteristic is $(+(cd - cd) - (cr - cr))$. (Note that the sign of the controlling characteristic is of no importance.)

A similar analysis can be made for for the "tens" digits (capital letters) and for the "hundreds" digits (italics) for these diagonals as well as for the other diagonals in these sections and for the main diagonals in the orthogonal sections parallel to the top and the front of the cube (see Figure 13–1).

Orthogonal Sections Parallel to the Left Side
    For x the controlling characteristic is $(cd - cd) \pm (cr - cr)$
    For X the controlling characteristic is $(cD - Cd) \pm (cR - Cr)$
    For *x* the controlling characteristic is $(cD - Cd) \pm (cR - Cr)$
Orthogonal Sections Parallel to the Top
    For x the controlling characteristic is $(rd - rd) \pm (cr - cr)$
    For X the controlling characteristic is $(rD - Rd) \pm (cR - Cr)$
    For *x* the controlling characteristic is $(rD - Rd) \pm (cR - Cr)$
Orthogonal Sections Parallel to the Front
    For x the controlling characteristic is $(rd - rd) \pm (cd - cd)$
    For X the controlling characteristic is $(rD - Rd) \pm (cD - Cd)$
    For *x* the controlling characteristic is $(rD - Rd) \pm (cD - Cd)$

FIGURE 13–1. CONTROLLING CHARACTERISTICS OF THE MAIN DIAGONALS

It remains to consider the space diagonals of the main cube. We shall again examine first the "units" digit for the following space diagonal:

$x \equiv (0(rd - rd) - 0(cd - cd) + 0(cr - cr))/\Delta \quad \text{mod } N$

$x \equiv (1(rd - rd) - 1(cd - cd) + 1(cr - cr))/\Delta \quad \text{mod } N$

$x \equiv (2(rd - rd) - 2(cd - cd) + 2(cr - cr))/\Delta \quad \text{mod } N$

. . . .

$x \equiv ((N - 1)(rd - rd) - (N - 1)(cd - cd) + (N - 1)(cr - cr))/\Delta \quad \text{mod } N$

Here each number in the sequence is

$$((rd - rd) - (cd - cd) + (cr - cr))/\Delta \quad \text{mod } N$$

greater than the preceding one. It follows that for this particular space diagonal the controlling characteristic is $((rd - rd) - (cd - cd) + (cr - cr))$. A similar analysis can be made for the "tens" digits (capital letters) and for the "hundreds" digits for this space diagonal, as well as for the other space diagonals (see Figure 13–2).

For x $\quad ((rd - rd) \pm (cd - cd) \pm (cr - cr))$
For X $\quad ((rD - Rd) \pm (cD - Cd) \pm (cR - Cr))$
For x $\quad ((rD - Rd) \pm (cD - Cd) \pm (cR - Cr))$

FIGURE 13–2. CONTROLLING CHARACTERISTICS OF THE SPACE DIAGONALS

It is thus seen that the values assigned to C, R, D, c, r, d, c, r, and d determine the magical properties of any given cube. It is convenient to refer to such a cube of order N as the

$$\begin{vmatrix} C & R & D \\ c & r & d \\ c & r & d \end{vmatrix}_N \quad \text{cube.}$$

Let us now investigate the conditions under which a cube can be made magic when one or more of the sets of orthogonals consist of N/s different capital (or lowercase, or italic) letters, each appearing s times where s is the greatest common divisor of the controlling characteristic and N. Another way of stating the problem is: let us investigate the conditions under which we can divide the numbers 1 to N—or what is the same thing, 0 to $(N - 1)$—inclusive, into s sets of N/s each, with all sets having the same total.

The average value of the numbers 0 to $(N-1)$, inclusive, is $1/N$th their total, or $(N-1)/2$. While this number is an integer when N is odd, it is a fraction when N is even. It follows therefore that when N is even and N/s is odd it is not possible to arrange the numbers 0 to $(N-1)$, inclusive, into s sets (of N/s numbers each) with all sets having the same total. Here we must resort to the expedient of transferring some of the numbers, as shown in Chapter 10.

What about when N and N/s are both even? This is quite easy. Form $N/2$ pairs of numbers as follows:

$$0 \qquad 1 \qquad 2 \qquad 3 \qquad 4 \quad \cdots \ (N/2-1)$$
$$(N-1)\ (N-2)\ (N-3)\ (N-4)\ (N-5) \ \cdots \quad N/2$$

Notice that the sum of the numbers forming each pair is $(N-1)$, or twice the value of the average value of a single term. It follows that by selecting $N/2s$ pairs of these numbers we will have a set of N/s numbers totaling $1/s$ of the total of 0 to $(N-1)$, inclusive. Picking s such sets may be done in many different ways.

In the case where N is odd, all factors must be odd and our problem reduces to whether when a and b are odd and $a \times b = N$ if the numbers 0 to $(N-1)$, inclusive, can be divided into a sets of b each, with each set having the same sum. The answer is yes.

With the exception of the middle term k, where $k=(N-1)/2$, the numbers 0 to $(N-1)$, inclusive, can be written as k pairs of numbers, each pair adding to $2k=(N-1)$, as follows:

$$0 \qquad 1 \qquad 2 \quad \cdots (k-i) \cdots (k-2)\ (k-1)$$
$$2k\ (2k-1)\ (2k-2) \cdots (k+i) \cdots (k+2)\ (k+1) \quad k$$

where i is any integer from 1 to k.

Let $j=(a-1)/2$ and select $3a$ numbers:

(1) The middle a numbers, namely, $(k-j)$ to $(k+j)$, inclusive,
(2) Any other a consecutive numbers, say $(k-i)$ to $(k-i+2j)$, inclusive, and
(3) The a consecutive numbers that are complementary to those just selected, namely, $(k+i-2j)$ to $(k+i)$, inclusive.

This will leave $(N-3a)/2$ pairs of complementary numbers available for future use. Now draw a rectangle having a columns and b rows. Insert the above three a numbers in the first three rows as follows:

$$
\begin{array}{cccccc}
(k-i) & (k-i+1) & \cdots & (k-i+j) & (k-i+j+1) & \cdots & (k-i+2j) \\
k & (k+1) & \cdots & (k+j) & (k-j) & \cdots & (k-1) \\
(k+i) & (k+i-2) & \cdots & (k+i-2j) & (k+i-1) & \cdots & (k+i-2j+1)
\end{array}
$$

The three numbers in any of the above columns add to $3k = 3(N-1)/2$. If we fill in the remaining $(b-3)$ cells in each column with $(b-3)/2$ of the complementary pairs of numbers at our disposal, which we can do in many different ways, each column will consist of b numbers whose sum will be $b(N-1)/2$, as required.

The above process looks quite formidable, but it actually is simple. Figure 13–3 shows one of the many ways we can partition the numbers 0 to 34, inclusive, into seven sets of five numbers, with the total of the numbers in each set being 85. Notice that the total of the first three numbers in each column is 51 and the total of the last two numbers in each column is 34. Needless to say, it would have been as easy to get five sets of seven each with a total of 119 per set.

4	5	6	7	8	9	10
17	18	19	20	14	15	16
30	28	26	24	29	27	25
23	3	22	2	21	1	0
11	31	12	32	13	33	34

FIGURE 13–3. PARTITIONING THE NUMBERS

In view of the above, it is apparent that—as long as Δ is prime to N and none of the controlling characteristics for the orthogonals are equal to 0—any intermediate cube of an odd order generated by the cyclical method can be made magic by the proper selection of values for the various letters. The ability to assign values to the letters in such a manner as to make any orthogonal or diagonal magic gives the method its great flexibility.

Chapter 14

Third-Order Magic Squares and Cubes

Richard Lewis Myers, Jr., proved that no normal third-order perfect cube could exist.[1] It only requires a slight modification of his proof to make it extend to third-order magic cubes formed of any numbers whatsoever. Myers used the square shown in Figure 14-1 in his proof and arrived at the statement that by adding together the numbers in the two diagonals and those in the center column you would get

$$3X + A + B + C + D + E + F = 3(42).$$

All we have to do is to replace the number 42 with the magic constant of the square, say K, where this constant may be any number, depending on the numbers composing the cube.

A	B	C
	X	
D	E	F

1. Martin Gardner discusses Myers' work in "Mathematical Games," *Scientific American* (January 1976), pp. 120, 122.

Continuing Myers' proof by subtracting from this equation the following one (based on the fact that each of the two horizontal orthogonals must add to the magic constant of the cube):

$$A + B + C + D + E + F = 2K$$

we will get:

$$3X = K$$

or

$$X = K/3.$$

The rest of Myers' proof is essentially unchanged—you merely replace 14 by K/3, as was done in Chapter 3.

In order to prove that a third-order pandiagonal cube could not exist (regardless of the numbers composing it), it was necessary to use the fact that the number in the center cell of any third-order cube had to equal one-third the magic constant of the cube. We offer the following original proof.

A	B	C
D	E	F
G	H	I

Front

J	K	L
M	N	O
P	Q	R

Middle

S	T	U
V	W	X
Y	Z	&

Back

FIGURE 14–2. PROOF THAT A THIRD-ORDER PANDIAGONAL CUBE DOES NOT EXIST

Consider the cube in Figure 14–2 and add together the following orthogonals: B, E, H; T, W, Z; D, M, V; F, O, X; J, K, L; and P, Q, R; and the four space diagonals: A, N, &; C, N, Y; G, N, U; and I, N, S. The result will be 3N plus the sum of all twenty-seven numbers = 10K (where K is the magic constant of the cube). But the sum of all twenty-seven numbers must equal 9K. It follows that:

$$3N = K$$

or

$$N = K/3 = 1/3 \text{ the magic constant of the cube.}$$

Appendix

The Two-Dimension Cyclical Method for Constructing Magic Squares

As a first step let us identify the individual cells forming the square by the coordinate (x, y) where x and y equal 0, 1, 2, . . ., $(n-1)$ counting from the left to the right and from the bottom up. Figure A–1 gives the coordinates when n equals 5.

0,4	1,4	2,4	3,4	4,4
0,3	1,3	2,3	3,3	4,3
0,2	1,2	2,2	3,2	4,2
0,1	1,1	2,1	3,1	4,1
0,0	1,0	2,0	3,0	4,0

FIGURE A–1.

Since we shall be using cyclical steps, all coordinates that differ by an exact multiple of n are equivalent. In a fifth-order square this means simply that 14, 9, 4, -1, -6, -11, and so forth are all equivalent. As another example, in a seventh-order square 21, 14, 7, 0, -7, -14, and so on are all equivalent. Thus the cell $(14, -11)$ would be equivalent to the cell $(4, 4)$ in a fifth-order square and to $(0, 3)$ in a seventh-order square.

Reprinted from William H. Benson and Oswald Jacoby, *New Recreations with Magic Squares* (New York: Dover Publications, 1976), pp. 43–47.

More generally we see that if j and k are integers (positive or negative and not necessarily different) then:

$$(jn + x, kn + y) \text{ is equivalent to } (x, y).$$

The second step is to select four integers C, R, c, and r (positive or negative and not necessarily different) such that:

(1) Each one is greater than minus n and less than plus n.
(2) None are equal to zero.
(3) The difference $(Cr - cR)$ is prime to n. (Two integers are prime to each other when they have no common factor other than 1; it follows that 1 is prime to all other integers.)

In order to demonstrate our method let us consider the following two combinations of values for C, R, c, and r:

	Case 1	Case 2
C	$+2$	$+1$
R	$+1$	$+1$
c	-1	-1
r	-2	-2
$(Cr - cR)$	-3	-1

The construction, once the various constants have been selected, is actually quite simple. The easiest way to explain it is by example. We shall first construct magic squares of the fifth, eighth, and tenth order using the values of C, R, c, and r given in Case 1. Note particularly that these values, as well as $(Cr - cR)$, meet the above three requirements.

A unique feature of our method is that a very general intermediate square is first constructed by the aid of n series of pairs of letters (one of each pair being a capital letter and the other a lowercase letter), namely, the A series, the B series, ..., the N series. Each series in turn contains the n lowercase letters $a, b, c, \ldots, n$.

The first step in the actual construction is to generate this intermediate square by the use of one series of cyclical steps after another. Each individual cell is occupied by one of these pairs of letters in accordance with the following rules:

(1) The A series is started by placing the pair $[A + a]$ in any desired cell, say cell $(1, 0)$.

(2) The remaining pairs in the A series are located by taking a series of construction steps that we shall identify as the (C, R) step, consisting of C columns to the right (left when C is negative) and R rows up (down when R is negative) from the cell last filled. For Case 1, C is $+2$ and R is $+1$, so the step is two columns over to the right and one row up. In the case of a fifth-order square this will place $[A+b]$ in cell $(3, 1)$; $[A+c]$ in cell $(5, 2)$ or, what is the equivalent, $(0, 2)$; $[A+d]$ in cell $(2, 3)$; and $[A+e]$ in cell $(4, 4)$. This completes the A series. Note that if you attempted to take one more regular (C, R) step the next cell $(6, 5)$ or, what is the equivalent, $(1, 0)$ is already occupied by $[A+a]$.

(3) It is evident that a special move (which we shall refer to as a *cross-step*) is necessary to start the B series. This cross-step, the $(C+c, R+r)$ cross-step, consists of a step of $(C+c)$ columns to the right (left if $C+c$ is negative) and $(R+r)$ rows up (down if $R+r$ is negative). For Case 1, $C+c=+1$ and $R+r=-1$, so the cross-step is one column to the right and one row down. It follows that $[B+a]$ belongs in cell $(5, 3)$ or, what is the equivalent, $(0, 3)$. See Figure A–2 for the appearance of the square at this point.

(4) After the cross-step has located the first pair of the B series, continue with the regular (C, R) step until the B series is completed. At this point, start the C series by again taking the cross-step $(C+c, R+r)$. Figure A–3 shows the square at this point.

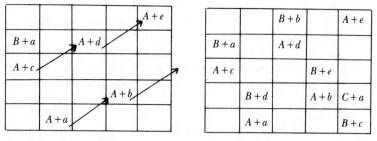

FIGURE A–2.   FIGURE A–3.

Repeat the above process until the square is completed, as shown in Figure A–4.

C+d	E+c	B+b	D+a	A+e
B+a	D+e	A+d	C+c	E+b
A+c	C+b	E+a	B+e	D+d
E+e	B+d	D+c	A+b	C+a
D+b	A+a	C+e	E+d	B+c

FIGURE A–4.

Notice that in each row, column, main diagonal, and broken diagonal the letters A, B, C, D, and E appear only once. Also note that the letters a, b, c, d, and e appear only once. In other words, if numerical values are assigned to these letters, the resultant square will be pandiagonal regardless of the values selected. Suppose, for example, that we desired to construct a pandiagonal magic square whose bottom row consisted of π to eight decimals. If you let $A = 10$, $B = 40$, $C = 14$, $D = 0$, $E = 90$, $a = 4$, $b = 3$, $c = 25$, $d = 2$, and $e = 1$, and substitute these values in Figure A–4, you will generate the pandiagonal (but not normal) magic square shown in Figure A–5.

16	115	43	4	11
44	1	12	39	93
35	17	94	41	2
91	42	25	13	18
3	14	15	92	65

FIGURE A–5. $\pi = 3.14159265!!!$

Usually we are interested in normal magic squares, that is, magic squares formed of the first n^2 natural numbers. The requirements to be met to ensure this property are quite simple:

(1) The capital letters A, B, C, D, . . . , N must be assigned values from:

(a) either the set 0, n, $2n$, $3n$, . . . , $(n-1)n$, or

(b) the set 1, 2, 3, 4, . . . , n.

(2) The lowercase letters a, b, c, d, . . . , n must be assigned values from:

(a) the set 1, 2, 3, 4, . . . , n whenever the capital letters are assigned values from the set 0, n, $2n$, $3n$, . . . , $(n-1)n$, or

(b) the set 0, n, $2n$, $3n$, . . . , $(n-1)n$ whenever the capital letters are assigned values from the set 1, 2, 3, 4, . . . , n.

It is absolutely immaterial in what order you assign these values as long as you assign each one once and only once. In all cases you will generate a normal pandiagonal magic square.

In the case of a fifth-order square these values become:

(1) the capital letters 0, 5, 10, 15, and 20 and the lowercase letters 1, 2, 3, 4, and 5, or

(2) the capital letters 1, 2, 3, 4, and 5 and the lowercase letters 0, 5, 10, 15 and 20.

A CATALOGUE OF SELECTED DOVER BOOKS IN ALL FIELDS OF INTEREST

CELESTIAL OBJECTS FOR COMMON TELESCOPES, T. W. Webb. The most used book in amateur astronomy: inestimable aid for locating and identifying nearly 4,000 celestial objects. Edited, updated by Margaret W. Mayall. 77 illustrations. Total of 645pp. 5⅜ x 8½.
20917-2, 20918-0 Pa., Two-vol. set $9.00

HISTORICAL STUDIES IN THE LANGUAGE OF CHEMISTRY, M. P. Crosland. The important part language has played in the development of chemistry from the symbolism of alchemy to the adoption of systematic nomenclature in 1892. ". . . wholeheartedly recommended,"—Science. 15 illustrations. 416pp. of text. 5⅝ x 8¼. 63702-6 Pa. $6.00

BURNHAM'S CELESTIAL HANDBOOK, Robert Burnham, Jr. Thorough, readable guide to the stars beyond our solar system. Exhaustive treatment, fully illustrated. Breakdown is alphabetical by constellation: Andromeda to Cetus in Vol. 1; Chamaeleon to Orion in Vol. 2; and Pavo to Vulpecula in Vol. 3. Hundreds of illustrations. Total of about 2000pp. 6⅛ x 9¼.
23567-X, 23568-8, 23673-0 Pa., Three-vol. set $26.85

THEORY OF WING SECTIONS: INCLUDING A SUMMARY OF AIR-FOIL DATA, Ira H. Abbott and A. E. von Doenhoff. Concise compilation of subatomic aerodynamic characteristics of modern NASA wing sections, plus description of theory. 350pp. of tables. 693pp. 5⅜ x 8½.
60586-8 Pa. $7.00

DE RE METALLICA, Georgius Agricola. Translated by Herbert C. Hoover and Lou H. Hoover. The famous Hoover translation of greatest treatise on technological chemistry, engineering, geology, mining of early modern times (1556). All 289 original woodcuts. 638pp. 6¾ x 11.
60006-8 Clothbd. $17.95

THE ORIGIN OF CONTINENTS AND OCEANS, Alfred Wegener. One of the most influential, most controversial books in science, the classic statement for continental drift. Full 1966 translation of Wegener's final (1929) version. 64 illustrations. 246pp. 5⅜ x 8½. 61708-4 Pa. $4.50

THE PRINCIPLES OF PSYCHOLOGY, William James. Famous long course complete, unabridged. Stream of thought, time perception, memory, experimental methods; great work decades ahead of its time. Still valid, useful; read in many classes. 94 figures. Total of 1391pp. 5⅜ x 8½.
20381-6, 20382-4 Pa., Two-vol. set $13.00

YUCATAN BEFORE AND AFTER THE CONQUEST, Diego de Landa. First English translation of basic book in Maya studies, the only significant account of Yucatan written in the early post-Conquest era. Translated by distinguished Maya scholar William Gates. Appendices, introduction, 4 maps and over 120 illustrations added by translator. 162pp. 5⅜ x 8½.
23622-6 Pa. $3.00

THE MALAY ARCHIPELAGO, Alfred R. Wallace. Spirited travel account by one of founders of modern biology. Touches on zoology, botany, ethnography, geography, and geology. 62 illustrations, maps. 515pp. 5⅜ x 8½.
20187-2 Pa. $6.95

THE DISCOVERY OF THE TOMB OF TUTANKHAMEN, Howard Carter, A. C. Mace. Accompany Carter in the thrill of discovery, as ruined passage suddenly reveals unique, untouched, fabulously rich tomb. Fascinating account, with 106 illustrations. New introduction by J. M. White. Total of 382pp. 5⅜ x 8½. (Available in U.S. only)   23500-9 Pa. $4.00

THE WORLD'S GREATEST SPEECHES, edited by Lewis Copeland and Lawrence W. Lamm. Vast collection of 278 speeches from Greeks up to present. Powerful and effective models; unique look at history. Revised to 1970. Indices. 842pp. 5⅜ x 8½.   20468-5 Pa. $8.95

THE 100 GREATEST ADVERTISEMENTS, Julian Watkins. The priceless ingredient; His master's voice; 99 44/100% pure; over 100 others. How they were written, their impact, etc. Remarkable record. 130 illustrations. 233pp. 7⅞ x 10 3/5.   20540-1 Pa. $5.00

CRUICKSHANK PRINTS FOR HAND COLORING, George Cruickshank. 18 illustrations, one side of a page, on fine-quality paper suitable for watercolors. Caricatures of people in society (c. 1820) full of trenchant wit. Very large format. 32pp. 11 x 16.   23684-6 Pa. $5.00

THIRTY-TWO COLOR POSTCARDS OF TWENTIETH-CENTURY AMERICAN ART, Whitney Museum of American Art. Reproduced in full color in postcard form are 31 art works and one shot of the museum. Calder, Hopper, Rauschenberg, others. Detachable. 16pp. 8¼ x 11.
23629-3 Pa. $2.50

MUSIC OF THE SPHERES: THE MATERIAL UNIVERSE FROM ATOM TO QUASAR SIMPLY EXPLAINED, Guy Murchie. Planets, stars, geology, atoms, radiation, relativity, quantum theory, light, antimatter, similar topics. 319 figures. 664pp. 5⅜ x 8½.
21809-0, 21810-4 Pa., Two-vol. set $10.00

EINSTEIN'S THEORY OF RELATIVITY, Max Born. Finest semi-technical account; covers Einstein, Lorentz, Minkowski, and others, with much detail, much explanation of ideas and math not readily available elsewhere on this level. For student, non-specialist. 376pp. 5⅜ x 8½.
60769-0 Pa. $4.50

SECOND PIATIGORSKY CUP, edited by Isaac Kashdan. One of the greatest tournament books ever produced in the English language. All 90 games of the 1966 tournament, annotated by players, most annotated by both players. Features Petrosian, Spassky, Fischer, Larsen, six others. 228pp. 5⅜ x 8½.   23572-6 Pa. $3.50

ENCYCLOPEDIA OF CARD TRICKS, revised and edited by Jean Hugard. How to perform over 600 card tricks, devised by the world's greatest magicians: impromptus, spelling tricks, key cards, using special packs, much, much more. Additional chapter on card technique. 66 illustrations. 402pp. 5⅜ x 8½. (Available in U.S. only)   21252-1 Pa. $3.95

MAGIC: STAGE ILLUSIONS, SPECIAL EFFECTS AND TRICK PHO-TOGRAPHY, Albert A. Hopkins, Henry R. Evans. One of the great classics; fullest, most authorative explanation of vanishing lady, levitations, scores of other great stage effects. Also small magic, automata, stunts. 446 illus-trations. 556pp. 5⅜ x 8½.   23344-8 Pa. $6.95

THE SECRETS OF HOUDINI, J. C. Cannell. Classic study of Houdini's incredible magic, exposing closely-kept professional secrets and revealing, in general terms, the whole art of stage magic. 67 illustrations. 279pp. 5⅜ x 8½.   22913-0 Pa. $3.00

HOFFMANN'S MODERN MAGIC, Professor Hoffmann. One of the best, and best-known, magicians' manuals of the past century. Hundreds of tricks from card tricks and simple sleight of hand to elaborate illusions involving construction of complicated machinery. 332 illustrations. 563pp. 5⅜ x 8½.   23623-4 Pa. $6.00

MADAME PRUNIER'S FISH COOKERY BOOK, Mme. S. B. Prunier. More than 1000 recipes from world famous Prunier's of Paris and London, specially adapted here for American kitchen. Grilled tournedos with anchovy butter, Lobster a la Bordelaise, Prunier's prized desserts, more. Glossary. 340pp. 5⅜ x 8½. (Available in U.S. only)   22679-4 Pa. $3.00

FRENCH COUNTRY COOKING FOR AMERICANS, Louis Diat. 500 easy-to-make, authentic provincial recipes compiled by former head chef at New York's Fitz-Carlton Hotel: onion soup, lamb stew, potato pie, more. 309pp. 5⅜ x 8½.   23665-X Pa. $3.95

SAUCES, FRENCH AND FAMOUS, Louis Diat. Complete book gives over 200 specific recipes: bechamel, Bordelaise, hollandaise, Cumberland, apri-cot, etc. Author was one of this century's finest chefs, originator of vichyssoise and many other dishes. Index. 156pp. 5⅜ x 8.
                                                    23663-3 Pa. $2.50

TOLL HOUSE TRIED AND TRUE RECIPES, Ruth Graves Wakefield. Authentic recipes from the famous Mass. restaurant: popovers, veal and ham loaf, Toll House baked beans, chocolate cake crumb pudding, much more. Many helpful hints. Nearly 700 recipes. Index. 376pp. 5⅜ x 8½.
                                                    23560-2 Pa. $4.50

AMERICAN ANTIQUE FURNITURE, Edgar G. Miller, Jr. The basic coverage of all American furniture before 1840: chapters per item chronologically cover all types of furniture, with more than 2100 photos. Total of 1106pp. 7⅞ x 10¾.   21599-7, 21600-4 Pa., Two-vol. set $17.90

ILLUSTRATED GUIDE TO SHAKER FURNITURE, Robert Meader. Director, Shaker Museum, Old Chatham, presents up-to-date coverage of all furniture and appurtenances, with much on local styles not available elsewhere. 235 photos. 146pp. 9 x 12.   22819-3 Pa. $5.00

ORIENTAL RUGS, ANTIQUE AND MODERN, Walter A. Hawley. Persia, Turkey, Caucasus, Central Asia, China, other traditions. Best general survey of all aspects: styles and periods, manufacture, uses, symbols and their interpretation, and identification. 96 illustrations, 11 in color. 320pp. 6⅛ x 9¼.   22366-3 Pa. $6.95

CHINESE POTTERY AND PORCELAIN, R. L. Hobson. Detailed descriptions and analyses by former Keeper of the Department of Oriental Antiquities and Ethnography at the British Museum. Covers hundreds of pieces from primitive times to 1915. Still the standard text for most periods. 136 plates, 40 in full color. Total of 750pp. 5⅜ x 8½.
23253-0 Pa. $10.00

THE WARES OF THE MING DYNASTY, R. L. Hobson. Foremost scholar examines and illustrates many varieties of Ming (1368-1644). Famous blue and white, polychrome, lesser-known styles and shapes. 117 illustrations, 9 full color, of outstanding pieces. Total of 263pp. 6⅛ x 9¼. (Available in U.S. only)   23652-8 Pa. $6.00